Praise for *Becoming the New Boss*

~

"It is clear that Dr. Hoff knows what it means to be a leader, and the distinction between leadership and management. Whether you are a new or experienced leader, your leadership will be improved by reading this book. It offers both practical and emotional insights, with the knowledge that leadership is about relationships and integrity."

DR. BRIAN G. RICCA, SUPERINTENDENT OF SCHOOLS, MONTPELIER PUBLIC SCHOOLS

"In this book Naphtali Hoff gives focused, practical guidance to seasoned and newly minted leaders alike. By being attuned to the leadership issues that lurk just beneath the surface, and proactively addressing them with his sage advice, we can establish a foundation for success in any new leadership role."

JUSTIN BAEDER, DIRECTOR OF THE PRINCIPAL CENTER

"Another book on leadership? Really? Well, please do yourself the favor of reading Naphtali Hoff's Becoming the New Boss, a wonderful synthesis of modern leadership theory along with the author's truly insightful commentary and insights. As a long-time school head, I am constantly immersed in leadership books and essays. What this work did for me was to pull it all together in a way both practical and motivational. I immediately began planning my leadership team's annual retreat with this work as the foundation. Thank you Naphtali!"

SCOTT WILSON, HEADMASTER OF BAYLOR SCHOOL, CHATTANOOGA, TN

"It's pretty easy to spot bad leadership—but do you know the tenets of good leadership? In Becoming the New Boss, *Naphtali Hoff, PsyD explains the differences between leadership and management in a conversational and easy reading style. Lots of anecdotes put his teachings into a real life construct for the reader, making it very possible to envision themselves in just that same position.*

This is a great guideline for new leaders—whether you have the position yet or not. Not only should current senior leadership read the book but also take the time to encourage their direct reports to as well.

> *"Many people think leadership is about rank, power, and privilege. Marines, however, maintain that true leadership is the willingness to place others' needs above your own."*

I like this book so much because Dr. Hoff's philosophy on leadership so closely matches my own. I've often told my teams, "when the spotlight comes on I will step out of the way, but if it turns out the light is really the headlights of an oncoming bus—they'll have to go through me first.

Though much of Naphtali's examples stem from his years in academia, the tenets he teaches can be translated to any number of industries. I'll be sending a copy to my adult children, one of which is a software engineer, the other a data scientist."

MELODY MCBETH, FOUNDER & PRINCIPAL, HIGHLAND FUNDRAISING SOLUTIONS, AUTHOR OF US UNIFORMED SERVICES GUIDE TO RANKS

"This book is a clear, direct, insightful explication of what those who would be leaders ought to read, ingest, and make part of their daily practice."

DR. MICHAEL LLORENZ, PROFESSOR OF MANAGEMENT, GRADUATE SCHOOL OF BUSINESS, TOURO COLLEGE AND UNIVERSITY SYSTEM

BECOMING THE
NEW
B♦SS

THE NEW LEADER'S
GUIDE TO
SUSTAINED SUCCESS

Naphtali Hoff, PsyD

INDIE BOOKS
INTERNATIONAL

No part of this publication may be reproduced or distributed in any form or by any means without the prior permission of the publisher. Requests for permission should be directed to permissions@indiebooksintl.com, or mailed to Permissions, Indie Books International, 2424 Vista Way, Suite 316, Oceanside, CA 92054.

Neither the publisher nor the author is engaged in rendering legal or other professional services through this book. If expert assistance is required, the services of appropriate professionals should be sought. The publisher and the author shall have neither liability nor responsibility to any person or entity with respect to any loss or damage caused directly or indirectly by the information in this publication.

ISBN-10: 1-941870-94-5
ISBN-13: 978-1-941870-94-5
Library of Congress Control Number: 2017941436

Designed by Joni McPherson, mcphersongraphics.com

INDIE BOOKS INTERNATIONAL, LLC
2424 VISTA WAY, SUITE 316
OCEANSIDE, CA 92054
www.indiebooksintl.com

Dedication

~

This book is dedicated to my wife Karyn, who has supported me through thick and thin, and to my children, Binyomin, Doniel, Shaina, Chaim, Malka, and Anshel, whom I love with every fiber of my being.

TABLE OF CONTENTS

Foreword

~

Becoming a new boss is a job filled with fear, uncertainty, and doubt. In the last five decades, I have had to step into the role of the new boss many times in many fields.

Along the way, I wish I had a book with the depth of knowledge that you now hold in your hands. Leadership effectiveness expert Naphtali Hoff has researched what a new leader needs to know to succeed. Now it is my honor to publish such a book.

His passion for leadership began during his leadership journey, which included administrative posts in multiple schools. Naphtali's personal experience in the leadership field allows him to understand leaders' needs and craft solutions to help them optimize their performance and success.

Today he is an executive coach who works with leaders who want to increase their leadership capacity and improve their team's effectiveness. He speaks and coaches hundreds of executives and leaders each year on how to increase productivity and engagement.

Any leader in a new position has many questions. And this book provides a depth of answers.

If you are an employee transitioning into your first leadership position or strongly considering it, this book will help with these questions:

- How do I position myself to make my move up?

- What key things do I have to consider in this transition?

- How do I gain quick acceptance and sustained success?

If you are a mid-level manager seeking that first executive level position, this book will help with these questions:

- How do I position myself to take the next step?

- What are the main differences between my current and aspired roles?

- What new skills will I need to develop?

If you are an executive transitioning to a new leadership opportunity, this book will help with these questions:

- How do I position myself to get hired or recruited?

- Which experiences can I bring along with me from my old job and which should I leave behind?

- How do I ensure sustained success?

Wherever you are on your leadership journey, congratulations on finding a guidebook that will help you make the trip a success. Best wishes for good reading and good leading.

Excelsior,

Henry DeVries, CEO, Indie Books International
Co-author of *How to Close a Deal Like Warren Buffett*

INTRODUCTION

A New Experience

Experience is the name everyone gives to their mistakes.

OSCAR WILDE

~

Congratulations! Your recent promotion to a position of leadership may very well represent the most exciting moment in your professional career. As an executive, you will have the opportunity to impact your organization and its employees on many levels, and to serve as a primary catalyst for its future growth and success.

In this role, you will be able to implement your vision and your dreams. Now, instead of following others' directions, you will give them. You have also "made it" and will now enjoy many financial as well as social benefits, such as the increased respect and attention that go along with your new post.

While leading others can be very exciting and fulfilling, you will likely also find it to be challenging, perhaps very much so. You will need to do a lot of learning to become familiar with your new position, your team, the workplace culture that you'll walk into, and what needs to happen for you to be successful. This new job places you on a different plane, with tasks and responsibilities that can be more demanding and stress-inducing than anything that you have ever before experienced at work.

Trust me. I have been there.

~

I had just signed on to become principal of an elementary school in a new community following more than a decade as a teacher and second-tier administrator. Though I had done much to ready myself for this moment, I had mixed feelings. On the one hand, I was a pretty confident guy and believed that I deserved this new job. I had worked hard through the years and felt that my abilities would hold me in good stead. I was excited about the opportunities that top-level leadership offered, particularly in a school setting where I could positively impact the lives of hundreds of children, their families, and their community.

And yet, I was also uneasy and unsure. My new job included many responsibilities that I had never been required to meet, at least not at this level. Sure, I had had superiors before, but I had never reported to a full board of directors, not to mention my many new unofficial bosses, such as parents and community leaders. And yes, I had previously managed staff. But they had been a small group of part-time teachers; nowhere near the fifty-plus members of my new, predominantly full-time faculty.

Perhaps most importantly, I was filling the shoes of a decorated principal: a man who had built his fledgling school, housed in a small strip mall, into a National Blue Ribbon School of Excellence with nearly 350 students. He was well loved and respected, an elderly gentleman with a grandfatherly persona and robust energy. He had retired under challenging conditions; his wife was diagnosed with a terminal illness from which she passed before the school year ended. The school community needed time to heal, let alone to get acclimated to a new sheriff.

At the same time, my predecessor's exit also fostered new hopes from those in the school community who had been pining for changes and improvements in recent years. These people included a number of board members and those on the head search committee. They had waited—many impatiently—for the day that a new change agent would be brought in to address their concerns. This was made very clear to me during the interview process and in informal conversation.

The fact that I entered the new position under such conditions certainly complicated things for me. Nor was my situation simplified by the fact that I was relocating to a new community together with my family and would have four of my own children at the school.

So many questions gnawed at me.

- How could I gain acceptance and respect?
- What should I do to demonstrate capacity without turning the entire school on its head?

- How might I shore up my weaker areas without showing frailty?

- Who would I turn to when things got rough for my family or me?

- Perhaps most importantly, had I made the right move in uprooting my family from the comfort of the life that we had built to start from scratch in a new community over 700 miles away?

Needless to say, it was not all smooth sailing from there. I took my lumps and more than once had to shift into some form of damage control. Despite the early struggles and learning pains, my time at this school was rewarding in many ways. We accomplished much in such areas as mission clarification, curriculum enhancement, professional development, teacher supervision, student assessment, positive behavior programming, communication, public relations, fiduciary oversight, and more.

None of this could have happened had I not learned from my mistakes and changed course. As I gained experience, I began to learn how better to galvanize our forces. Instead of trying to be a one-man tour de force, I learned to how to listen better and lead our talented team of administrators, faculty, and lay leaders in the pursuit of our strategic priorities.

To illustrate, I would like to share an old story that you may have heard about a reporter who was interviewing a successful bank president. He wanted to know the secret of the man's success. "Two words," he was told; "right decisions."

"And how do you make right decisions?" asked the reporter.

The reply: "One word. Experience."

The reporter pressed on. "And how do you get experience?" he asked.

To which the banker replied, "Two words: Wrong decisions."

My goal in writing this volume is to help you gain the benefits of experience without having to make too many bad decisions along the way. In the coming chapters, I will share many of the approaches that helped me navigate through my difficult beginning and lead our school into its next phase of success. Mind you, some of these took time to learn and refine. I often reflect on how much easier things may have been had I known more about them earlier on. That is why I wrote this book; so that other new leaders can hit the ground running.

In the pages that follow, we will explore together some of the most important leadership issues with which new leaders grapple. These include:

- The essence of leadership, and how it differs from management
- The importance of developing a leadership character
- How to make a great impression and start off on the right foot
- Ways to develop deep, balanced workplace relationships
- When and how to approach change
- Strategies to avoid burnout
- And much more

Remember, as a new leader you have a great opportunity in front of you to guide, direct and inspire others to new heights. But no great leader can go it alone, especially at the beginning.

It is my hope in writing this book is to provide you, the new leader, with tools, guidance, and support that will help you make a low-turbulence, high-reward leadership transition that often evades new leaders.

SECTION 1

UNDERSTANDING THE LEADER'S ROLE

CHAPTER 1

What's All the Fuss about Leadership, and What Is It Anyway?

Leadership is influence; nothing more, nothing less.

JOHN C. MAXWELL

Perhaps more so than in any era of human history, modern society has placed a pronounced emphasis on the study of human leadership. Few foci have consumed the collective interest of university researchers, think tanks, executive coaches, organizational consultants, business magnates, and internet bloggers more than identifying the special mix of qualities and actions that produce and sustain strong headship.

The topic's currency is obvious enough. At no time in our historical annals has there been a greater demand for capable, dynamic leadership—at least on such broad a scale—as there is today. Modern society has engendered the vast proliferation of large organizational structures, including governments, business corporations, and educational institutions. Each of these entities depends heavily on the skills and successes of key leaders to drive their enterprises forward.

Great leaders increase profit, drive up customer satisfaction, generate higher levels of engagement in their employees, reduce employee turnover, and develop stronger employees.[1] Logically, organizations make the study and recruitment of effective management an essential, ongoing effort, and invest heavily in programs and services to nurture and assess their chief executives.

---

[1] Zenger, John H., Joseph R. Folkman, Robert H. Sherwin Jr., and Barbara A. Steel. *How to Be Exceptional: Drive Leadership Success by Magnifying Your Strengths*. New York: McGraw-Hill, 2012.

As I see it, leadership matters today more than ever before, in part for the following reasons.

- **Shifting, less structured marketplace.** Today's work environment is more agile, dexterous, and virtual than ever before, with many offsite employees and less emphasis on traditional reporting and organizational hierarchies. Leading becomes more challenging in less structured environments.

- **Navigating in unchartered waters.** We live in a time of constant change, with an ever-increasing demand for product development and acceptance in a fast-paced global economy.

- **Heightened expectations.** Today's stakeholders are better informed and more demanding. They are less inclined to tolerate incompetence and wait patiently for evidence of success. Leaders today are expected to hit the ground running, but do so with short leashes.

- **Too many failures.** We have all observed longstanding bastions of stability, such as government and big business, fail before our eyes. Traditional organizational values have come under fierce attack, and we often seem to lack a moral compass by which to determine right and wrong.

These challenges, as well as many others, can make organizational leadership a daunting, perplex task, particularly for new leaders.

But what exactly is leadership?

In its essence, leadership comprises two primary, related components: social influence and the maximization of others' efforts. Influence is about winning people over to a new way of thinking and practice, through questioning, idea sharing, collaboration, and modeling. It emphasizes persuasion and motivation over coercion.

Influence occurs primarily through emotional connections, such as when we share triumphant or challenging times together. It also develops when leaders routinely demonstrate feelings of appreciation, care, concern, and empathy.

In a speech to graduating cadets at the Royal British Military Academy in 1944, General Dwight D. Eisenhower said: "You must know every single one of your men. It is not enough that you are the best soldier in that unit, that you are the strongest, the toughest, the most durable, the best equipped, technically—you must be their leader, their father, their mentor, even if you're half their age. You must understand their problems. You must keep them out of trouble; if they get in trouble, you must be the one who goes to their rescue. That cultivation of human understanding between you and your men is the one part that you must yet master, and you must master it quickly."

Clearly, this message has been embraced by the United States military as well. Simon Sinek is a best-selling author on team-building. He learned some of his core leadership beliefs from Lt. Gen. George Flynn, a United States Marine Corps official. Flynn was explaining what makes the Corps so extraordinarily tight-knit, to the point that they willingly entrust their lives to one another. He told Sinek that when Marines line up for their food each day, the most junior officers go first, following in rank order. Their leaders eat last. Such procedures are not recorded in the Marine Corps handbook or procedural code. Nor are they expressed at roll call. It's just the way that Marine leadership views their responsibility.

Many people think leadership is about rank, power, and privilege. Marines, however, maintain that true leadership is the willingness to place others' needs above your own. That's why Sinek titled his 2014 book *Leaders Eat Last: Why Some Teams Pull Together and Others Don't*.[2] True leadership, he writes, is about empowering others to achieve things they didn't believe possible.

By prioritizing the well-being of their people, exceptional organizations motivate their workers to give everything they've got to advance the organization. Peter Drucker once described it as, "lifting a person's vision to high sights... raising... a person's performance to a higher standard...(going) beyond its normal limitations."

$\sim$

In addition to the aforementioned qualities, strong leaders possess other attributes that help them achieve great success.

- **Driven.** Great leaders are driven. Drive is the engine that turns ideas into action and action into results. It also motivates us to forge

---

[2] Sinek, Simon. *Leaders Eat Last: Why Some Teams Pull Together and Others Don't*. Kbh.: Nota, 2014.

ahead, to advance in the face of opposition, disappointment, and setbacks, and to reach new levels of success.

- **Inspired.** Strong leaders are inspired leaders. They use their influence to guide, advise, and motivate their teams, helping their people see beyond the moment, and get past their perceived obstacles, false assumptions, and limiting beliefs.

> *Many people think leadership is about rank, power, and privilege. Marines, however, maintain that true leadership is the willingness to place others' needs above your own.*

- **Credible.** Productive leaders are credible, which means that others believe in them and their message. They are seen as experts in their field and deserve to be taken seriously. Such credibility does not develop overnight; it occurs when leaders regularly inspire trust in others and demonstrate great personal capacity.

- **Comfortable taking risk.** Leadership requires regular risk-taking. Everything from budgeting to staffing to programming carries some element of risk. This is certainly true for the more complex, hazardous tasks that define leadership, such as crafting a new vision and shifting course. Effective leaders understand that risk-taking is central to their jobs and are willing to make tough decisions as needed.

- **Build from strength.** Great leaders can pinpoint what they and their company do best and stay focused on building from strength. Steve Jobs, the late Apple CEO, found a company in dysfunction when he returned to Apple in 1997, twelve years after being fired. His extensive observations revealed a rudderless ship that lacked discipline and focus. Jobs called together his managers and told them to stop all production. He then drew a box with four quadrants. Over the two columns, he wrote "desktop" and "laptop." He labeled the two rows "home" and "business." He said that Apple would create the best products in each of those four categories and nothing more, at least for the time being. We all know how the story turned out from there.

CHAPTER 2

Lead, Don't Just Manage

You manage things; you lead people.

REAR ADMIRAL GRACE MURRAY HOPPER

$\sim$

The terms *leader* and *manager* are often used interchangeably. Are they the same? Most leadership experts say "no."

In *Leading Change,* Harvard professor John P. Kotter explains the difference as follows: "Management is a set of processes that keep an organization functioning...The processes are about planning, budgeting, staffing, clarifying jobs, measuring performance, and problem-solving when results did not go to plan," writes Kotter. "(Leadership, in contrast,) is about aligning people to the vision...(through) buy-in and communication, motivation and inspiration."[3]

To summarize, management is keeping things functioning in their current state, while leadership is about crafting and implementing a new vision.

Along these same lines, leadership consultant Warren Bennis composed a sizable list of distinctions between the role of the manager and the leader.[4] Some of these differences are:

- The manager administers; the leader innovates.
- The manager maintains; the leader develops.
- The manager focuses on systems and structure; the leader focuses on people.
- The manager relies on control; the leader inspires trust.
- The manager has a short-range view; the leader has a long-range perspective.

---

[3] Kotter, John P. *Leading Change*. Boston, MA: Harvard Business School Press, 1996. P. 25
[4] Bennis, Warren G. *On Becoming a Leader*. Reading, MA: Addison-Wesley Pub., 1989: 42.

- The manager asks how and when; the leader asks what and why.

- The manager has his or her eye on the bottom line; the leader's eye is on the horizon.

- The manager accepts the status quo; the leader challenges it.

- The manager does things right; the leader does the right thing.

According to Abraham Zaleznik, the late professor of leadership at Harvard Business School, these two styles emerge from the amount of structure on which people thrive. Managers, he wrote, embrace process, stability, and control.[5] They instinctively try to resolve problems quickly, sometimes at the expense of appreciating their full significance and addressing them properly for the long haul. In contrast, Zaleznik saw in leaders a willingness to tolerate a lack of structure. They are prepared to keep answers and solutions in suspense, avoiding premature closure on important issues; this keeps them open to new possibilities and ways of thinking.

If you have taken the Myers-Briggs Type Indicator (MBTI), a personality test, you may be familiar with the distinction that the test makes between those who prefer "judging" (J) or "perceiving" (P).

The Swiss psychiatrist Carl Jung developed these classifications in the early 1930s. Jung believed that all humans are born with a preference for one of two basic cognitive information-processing functions:

1. **A judging function**: The ability to reflect upon information and to organize it in such a way as to understand it and to then make decisions.

2. **A perceiving function**: The ability to gather, store and retrieve information by observing the world around them as well as their own memories and inner states.

Js (Judgers) typically align with our manager profile, preferring to get things decided quickly. In contrast, Ps (Perceivers) would rather stay open to new information and options than make a final decision, which is a key quality of leadership.

Statistics from the Myers and Briggs Foundation indicate that, when measured

---

[5] Zaleznik, Abraham. "Managers and Leaders: Are They Different?" *Clinical Leadership & Management Review: The Journal of CLMA* 18, no. 3 (2004): 171.

across the board, those who identify as "judging" are more common than those who generally "perceive" by a 54 percent to 46 percent margin. Folks in leadership and management positions combined to identify as *J* nearly 58 percent of the time,[6] which means that most administrators tend to want to focus on the here and now and not rock their respective boats.

A leader's behaviors are not necessarily bound by his or her type indicator. *J*s are certainly capable of taking a longer-term view on problems, but it requires more effort and perhaps more external assistance, such as from a coach, than *P*s might require. In contrast, *P*s may need extra assistance in managing the moment while they plan the future.

Leaders who understand their type preferences can more easily identify their strengths and potential weaknesses, develop self-awareness and emotional intelligence, and understand the impact of their behaviors on others.

This is not to suggest that we must replace all management with leadership. The two serve different, yet essential, purposes. In fact, most of us need to engage in both to ensure effective organizational function. The key for anyone in a leadership position is to be cognizant of when they are engaged in each aspect of their jobs and to aspire to be a leader first and foremost.

To again quote Kotter: "We need superb management. And we need more superb leadership. We need to be able to make our complex organizations reliable and efficient. We need them to jump into the future—the right future—at an accelerated pace, no matter the size of the changes required to make that happen."[7]

It is through management that companies implement the ideas, actions, and processes that lead to success. Leaders, however, are the ones that first develop the plan and chart the course for success. They also inspire their teams to take the necessary actions to ensure that their visions are actualized. The late Stephen Covey expressed the difference as follows: "Management is efficiency in climbing the ladder of success; leadership determines whether the ladder is leaning against the right wall."[8]

$\sim$

---

[6] Based on a study of nearly 26,500 persons at the Center for Creative Leadership.

[7] Kotter, John P. "Management Is (Still) Not Leadership." *Harvard Business Review*. August 07, 2014. Accessed February 22, 2017. http://blogs.hbr.org/2013/01/management-is-still-not-leadership/.

[8] Covey, Stephen R. *The Seven Habits of Highly Effective People: Restoring the Character Ethic*. New York: Simon and Schuster, 1989: 101.

I have observed that it is particularly easy for new leaders to fall into a management trap, even when they walk into well-oiled environments. Without question, process oversight is easier than visioning, particularly at the beginning when everything still has to be learned. Management requires less collaboration and less change, which means less disruption

> *Leaders, however, are the ones that first develop the plan and chart the course for success. They also inspire their teams to take the necessary actions to ensure that their visions are actualized.*

of daily routines. People who manage also feel like they're getting something done right away, which helps to secure some early wins.

Certainly, it takes time to get acclimated and, as we will discuss below, it would be wise to keep change on the back-burner during your first weeks and months on the job. Still, I suggest that you approach all of your learning and interactions from a leader's mindset, thinking about what could be, getting people excited about new possibilities as you go.

CHAPTER 3

Build a Leadership Character

Nearly all men can stand adversity, but if you want to
test a man's character, give him power.

ABRAHAM LINCOLN

~

In contemporary contexts, we have increasingly come to think of leaders as well-positioned people with strong connections. These men and women are in ample possession of intellect, charisma, power, and wealth. More often than not, we judge them (and they judge themselves) by what they have, or what they have been able to achieve in advancing their institution's bottom line. (Of course, one primary downside to this way of thinking, in addition to the fact that it is fundamentally flawed, is that because few people have great charisma or these other qualities, we conclude that few people can provide genuine leadership.)

Rare are the leaders whom we view primarily by their character and deeds, not to mention the qualitative impact they make on others around them. Not surprisingly, then, many leaders today focus more on what they can get from their positions of authority rather than on what they can give to the institutions and people they lead.

Any attempt to define and portray leadership without discussing character is both limited and limiting. Character fundamentally shapes how we engage with others around us, what we value and care about, the things we act on and reinforce, and how we arrive at decisions.

Research shows that the very best leaders, the ones who have been successful in elevating their organizations to the top of their respective fields, are individuals who prioritize and exemplify such qualities as selflessness, care, and consideration. They are humble and willing to admit error, on top of their other core managerial competencies that they possess.

In *From Good to Great*, Jim Collins describes his quest to identify the qualities that made certain high-profile companies particularly successful.[9] He and his research team began the process with a list of nearly 1500 corporations. Through the use of growth-related criteria,[10] they narrowed the list down to a group of eleven truly "great" corporations. Additional research revealed that all eleven companies had a few particular things in common, including the fact that they were all headed by what Collins termed *Level 5 Leaders*.

These leaders were all smart, shrewd, skilled, and knowledgeable of their respective products and market. They were effective at developing and managing teams within their organization, establishing a vision, setting goals, and meeting performance objectives. But so were many of the leaders of the 1500 other corporations in his study. What set these Level 5 CEOs apart from so many others in their peer group was the fact that they were recognized and admired by their coworkers for their noble character.

The Level 5 leaders were humble and did not pursue success for their personal glory. Some were quiet and introverted but remained undaunted when the need arose for them to make difficult (even risky) decisions. They were caring about others while also maintaining a burning, passionate drive—a deep desire to advance their respective cause. And because they were so exceptional in their care and concern, other leaders within their organizations began to mimic their deeds and thinking processes, which further advanced each respective company's cause.

For years, leadership programs and books have emphasized strength and decisiveness, believing that people wanted their leaders to be tough, courageous, knowledgeable, and self-confident. In contrast, humility, care, and other similar traits were not seen as desirable leadership qualities. After all, how could modest, self-effacing, think-of-others-first executives motivate workers and influence change?

A cursory review of some of the world's most successful leaders, however, presents the leadership profile in a very different light. Ancient leaders such as Abraham, Moses, and Jesus, as well as some more recent examples

---

[9] Collins, James C. *Good to Great: Why Some Companies Make the Leap...and Others Don't.* New York, NY: HarperBusiness, 2001.

[10] Their goal was to find every company that had made a leap from no-better-than-average results to great results (defined as generating cumulative stock returns that had exceeded the general stock market by at least three times over fifteen years. The leap had to also be independent of its industry). The eleven "good-to-great" companies averaged returns 6.9 times greater than the market's.

like Washington, Lincoln, Gandhi, and Mandela all moved mountains and shaped modern history without an abundance of charisma, heated rhetoric or an inflated sense of self-importance.

Genuine humility and care are indicators of a leader's inner strength, as well as his deep knowledge and self-fulfillment. Such leaders view their roles as opportunities to serve others. They can often better motivate others to listen and follow their example knowing that the leader is not motivated by glory, greed, and self-aggrandizement. Humble, caring leaders willingly acknowledge errors (theirs or their organization's) and change course as needed. It's never about them; the focus remains on getting the job done in the best way possible. When their actions or decisions are criticized, they remain open to change and growth. These leaders take pride in their achievements, but mainly as a platform to bring their people together to do even greater things.

Few have expressed it better than legendary University of Alabama former head football coach, Paul "Bear" Bryant. Bryant would often say, "If anything goes bad, I did it. If anything goes semi-good, we did it. If anything goes really good, then you did it."

CHAPTER 4

Learn to Think Like a Leader

Before you are a leader, success is all about growing yourself.
When you become a leader, success is all about growing others.

JACK WELCH

~

In the late 1990s, I was taking a methodology class as a requirement for teaching social studies. The class met at Roosevelt University's Schaumberg campus just outside Chicago. The instructor did a wonderful job helping us understand the importance of making history come alive for our students. We learned about developing engaging lessons with clear themes that promote student creativity. In general, it was once of the most useful and enjoyable graduate classes that I have attended.

During one class, the professor related a conversation that he had had with an executive at nearby Motorola. The topic of education had come up between the two men, and the executive had really laid into his professor friend. "You guys in education have it all wrong," he said. "You teach everyone to work alone and that communicating and sharing ideas is cheating. Once these kids get into the workplace, we need to completely deprogram and retrain them to cooperate and collaborate, to work together effectively." The professor, duly humbled, shared this powerful conversation with us. It was a concept that I held on to as I began my career in the field of education.

~

Too many new leaders also have it all wrong, at least regarding how we view our new roles. We think of leadership as the next step in our ascent, representing an increase in responsibility, authority, and prestige. But we do not necessarily see it as one that demands fundamental changes to our core thinking and behaviors. That is a mistake, for to assume a leadership post is to accept a whole new type of position than what we've held until then.

Before accepting this new job, attainment was all about you and your performance. You worked hard to achieve success and hoped that it would get you noticed and promoted. You invested time and effort in showcasing your contributions, with the understanding that your accomplishments would translate into you being able to take that next professional step.

Once you become a leader, however, achievement is measured mainly by your ability to grow others, to make those around you more capable, more confident, and more efficacious. The game is no longer about you winning. It's your team that must win for your term as a leader to be deemed a success.

No doubt, this paradigm shift can be much easier said than done. Since your youth, you have been encouraged to succeed as an individual. Sure, you were taught to be respectful of others and include them in social activities and school projects, but at the end of the day, it was about you. As you moved into the workplace, you brought that *me-first* attitude with you. Perhaps you were placed on a team and had to work with others to complete tasks. But were you genuinely invested in their success? If you are like most people, the answer is "no."

> *How you perform individually is of little consequence if the process falls behind schedule or comes in over budget. When your team wins, you win. When they stumble, the blame will find its way back to you.*

As a leader, that decades-old mindset needs to change, and in a hurry. In the words of the great industrialist Andrew Carnegie, "No man will make a great leader who wants to do it all himself, or to get all the credit for doing it."[11]

What can new leaders do to adjust their thinking and become more we-oriented? One primary consideration is to remember how your success will be measured. Keep a sticky note on your corkboard or a little sign on your desk that shares a message of cohesion and common goals. Something like:

- *"If everyone is moving forward together, then success takes care of itself."*
  —Henry Ford

---

[11] Quoted in Whitten, Neal. *Managing Software Development Projects: Formula for Success.* New York: Wiley, 1990: 63.

- *"Alone we can do so little; together we can do so much."* —Helen Keller

- *"We cannot accomplish all that we need to do without working together."* —Bill Richardson

Remember; as a leader, your primary role is to advance your team and to engage their collective talents toward achieving the goals that you have set. How you perform individually is of little consequence if the process falls behind schedule or comes in over budget. When your team wins, you win. When they stumble, the blame will find its way back to you.

Another strategy to keep you focused on "we" over "me" is to reflect upon the gift of leading. As we noted in the introduction, leadership offers leaders an opportunity to make a broad and deep impact on others and the organization. Leaders who remember this blessing and come to work each day with the goal of helping their team will find that they don't have the time or the interest to think much about themselves. They are simply too engrossed in the broader success of their endeavors to worry about personal gains. As the wise coaching adage goes, "focus on the process, forget the outcome." If the process is strong and we-oriented, the outcome will take care of itself, and everyone will win.

CHAPTER 5

Lead Ethically, from the Values Up

If a man's associates find him guilty of being phony, if they find that he lacks forthright integrity, he will fail.

DWIGHT D. EISENHOWER

~

I remember the comment as if it were yesterday. As a high school teacher, I had been invited to a school spirit Sabbath event for students and faculty at an area hotel. The facility sat on a sprawling property, and its layout was unconventional, to say the least, which made navigation from one place to another a bit challenging. At one point, I pointed the group that I was with in the wrong direction before someone realized the error. Not too pleased with his incompetent navigator, this guy quipped, "at least you weren't tasked to lead the Hebrews through the Sinai desert." Let's just say that I felt very un-Moses like at the moment.

We noted above that a key component of leadership is influence. Leaders understand that their role is to inspire others and lead them towards the desired outcome. But how can leaders themselves be sure that they have set off along the correct path, particularly when there appears to be more than one viable way forward?

One way is to lead from values. Values are the core components of a person's deepest beliefs, the concepts that they hold most dear. When a leader takes the time to identify her deepest values, she is likelier to remain consistent in her actions and decisions. Moreover, if she is effective in articulating her values, then others will understand her reasoning and, more often than not, be more inclined to support her process.

As leaders, we are given many opportunities to choose between possible actions and reactions. While we hopefully have our own values clearly articulated to drive such decision-making, our colleagues and coworkers don't always share those same values and priorities.

Creating a shared sense of values may not be as challenging as would first appear. For starters, gather your team together for a conversation. Offer them a values list.[12] Focus on company values and narrow down the list to a core group that can help direct future decision-making. Then, send the list around for clarification and confirmation. Once complete, publicize the list. At a future meeting, present scenarios so that everyone can discuss the situation in the context of the values that they have selected.

Say, for example, the company has embraced a respectful work environment that prioritizes personal well-being and family over the pursuit of profits. Present a scenario in which these values are threatened by such things as harsh, competitive marketplace conditions or demanding clients. Ask the group to identify the challenge to their values and how they would expect their leaders to respond. In this way, they will crystalize their position and be prepared when inevitable conflicts arise.

Recently, a Japanese manufacturer transitioned into its third generation of leadership. The founder's grandson who now runs the company discovered that because he was significantly younger than many of the company's managers, they were not willing to follow his leadership. The young CEO responded by establishing a dozen corporate values. Then he spent time working with team members to ensure understanding of and respect for the values. He regularly tells his managers, "We don't make decisions based on what I say; we make them based on what the values say." And they listen better as a result.[13]

Values-based leadership begins with the leader. You cannot expect your team to perform with character and integrity without first setting the example. Your team looks to you as a leader for guidance and direction. You must know and have the capacity to articulate your own values as well as your

---

[12] Such as this one: "What Are Your Values?: Deciding What's Most Important in Life." Decision-Making Skills from MindTools.com. Accessed February 22, 2017. http://www.mindtools.com/pages/article/newTED_85.htm.

[13] Shinobu Ishizuka: 2 Lessons from Japan's Values-Driven Companies." Benedictine University CVDL. September 01, 2015. Accessed February 22, 2017. http://www.cvdl.org/blog/shinobu-ishizuka-2-lessons-japans-values-driven-companies/

organization's values. And then you must live by them. What you do, not what you say, demonstrates most what you care about.

A reward system for team members who consistently act according to the company values will reinforce desired outcomes and give you a forum to promote positive conduct. Whenever possible, share the good word about what your colleagues have achieved or how they are walking the walk and enhancing your organization as a result.

> *Your team looks to you as a leader for guidance and direction. You must know and have the capacity to articulate your own values as well as your organization's values. And then you must live by them.*

It is also necessary to establish consequences for team members who don't follow the organization's values. We all strive to be good and act in accordance with our values. But sometimes we fall short and must be held accountable to prevent slippage.

CHAPTER 6

Put Your Vision on a Scale

In order to carry a positive action,
we must develop here a positive vision.
DALAI LAMA

～

Once I met with a group of my teachers to discuss an area of concern—student comportment. The teachers collectively felt that respect and responsibility were among some key areas of deficit within the student population and that something needed to be done about it. Without getting into details about how we approached the issue as a staff, we were able to get started on what could be an overwhelming task—defining and elevating the behavioral standard for over 350 children and the tens of staff that supported them—and make meaningful inroads towards a better outcome. This occurred because we were able to take an honest look at ourselves and our current situation, envision a better tomorrow, and identify the many steps that we needed to take to effect meaningful improvements.

One of the techniques that I enjoy using in my coaching and training work is a scaling exercise. It is a powerful process that offers a strong visual and emotional framework for individuals who seek change in their professional practice or some other area in their lives.

The first thing that I ask the client or workshop attendees to do is to describe the subject area on a scale from one to ten, with ten being the ideal and a one being the exact opposite. I ask for vivid descriptors that help create a clear vision of each extreme and also elicit from them some emotional terms that connect the individuals more deeply with each experience.

An example of this would be to scale internal communication within a company. What does a ten look and feel like? What does a one look and feel like? In the first case, I might get back such descriptive terms as "smooth,"

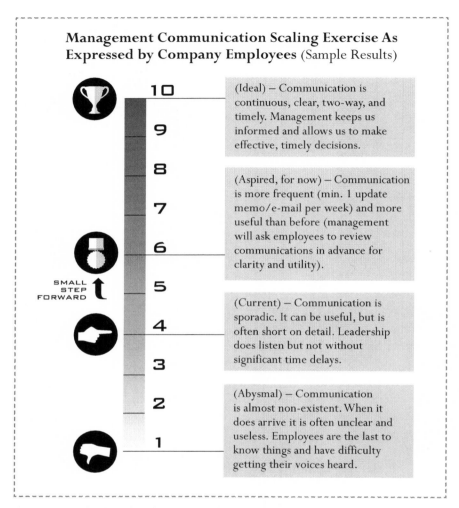

Management Communication Scaling Exercise As Expressed by Company Employees (Sample Results)

10	(Ideal) – Communication is continuous, clear, two-way, and timely. Management keeps us informed and allows us to make effective, timely decisions.
9	
8	(Aspired, for now) – Communication is more frequent (min. 1 update memo/e-mail per week) and more useful than before (management will ask employees to review communications in advance for clarity and utility).
7	
6	
SMALL STEP FORWARD 5	
4	(Current) – Communication is sporadic. It can be useful, but is often short on detail. Leadership does listen but not without significant time delays.
3	
2	(Abysmal) – Communication is almost non-existent. When it does arrive it is often unclear and useless. Employees are the last to know things and have difficulty getting their voices heard.
1	

"continuous," "clear," "relevant," and "timely," together with such feelings as "content," "informed," and "included." The lowest rung on the communicative ladder may be described as "infrequent," "ambiguous," "unimportant," and "isolated," making people feel disconnected and unhappy. By the time that we are done with this part of the process, we tend to be pretty clear on how to describe internal communication in its optimal form as well as when the organization is functioning at a dysfunctional level.

Once we have these bookend definitions in place, we then explore the current reality. I ask them, "If you were asked to scale your present situation, what score would you assign? Why?" This part of the scaling exercise can be particularly difficult, as it forces people to come to grips with their situation and also seek to identify the specific factors, such as systems, professional conduct, and the like, that are contributing to their less-than-optimal experience.

> *The scaling technique is very simple, at least in terms of establishing the end goals. Arriving at a clear, applicable vision will be harder.*

After this process is complete, I then ask those I am working with to think about a level of improvement that is within reach, such as going from a four to a five, or perhaps even a six. We talk about the specific components that separate the two levels and formulate an actionable plan, with quantifiable deliverables, which will help everybody know we have reached our goal or are at least trending in the right direction. We also establish a timeframe by which to achieve this growth so that the initial clarity and inspiration are not lost along the way. The net result is a plan that goes beyond griping about the present to agreeing to concrete steps that will result in progress.

In essence, the scaling technique is very simple, at least in terms of establishing the end goals. Arriving at a clear, applicable vision will be harder. The key to its success is a combination of identifying clear parameters of quality and honestly assessing the present situation. Once that is achieved, leaders and their teams can get to work on converting their vision into reality and making the workplace a more fulfilling and enjoyable space for all members of the team.

SECTION 2

LAYING THE FOUNDATION

CHAPTER 7

Do Your Homework

There's only one interview technique that matters...Do your homework so you can listen to the answers and react to them and ask follow-ups. Do your homework; prepare.

JIM LEHRER

~

My first leadership experience was the most unusual, most unexpected, and most fleeting managerial role that I ever held. As a high school senior, I was asked if I could provide kosher supervision at a Manhattan restaurant on Saturday nights. I didn't live too far from the place and wanted to earn some extra cash, so I agreed. The position, I was told, included oversight in the kitchen, and, because I could be in and out, manning the cash register.

The first night was going pretty smoothly. It took me a short while to learn the inner workings of the establishment's kitchen and how to operate the register. Not bad, I thought, for $10 an hour. But then, the head waiter told me that I had a phone call.

"Is this the manager?" asked the woman on the line.

"Manager?" I thought. I hesitated, thinking that he had called the wrong guy to the phone. I asked her to hold and went back to the head waiter. He explained to me that every kosher supervisor who works in that restaurant is also the manager. So yes, I was the right one to answer. I picked the phone back up.

The woman, by now confused and a bit annoyed, asked incredulously, "*Are you sure* that you're the manager?" With the confidence of a censored child, I meekly replied in the affirmative.

Let's just say that I've had better leadership moments than that one.

~

Most new leaders accept their first leadership posts with a superior understanding of their job responsibilities than I did. But too many still do not know enough about their new job before they start their positions. This may happen because they received a vague job description, competing sets of marching orders from recruiters, potential bosses and/or search committee members, limited opportunity to meet and engage with current employees, or a combination thereof.

What can aspiring leaders do to ensure that they operate in their new roles with maximal clarity from day one? The following strategies can help.

- **Review the job description thoroughly before applying.** In most cases, detailed job descriptions are available to potential applicants. Review the core job expectations and ask yourself if you are comfortable with everything that is listed. If not, make a note to explore those areas in particular during the interview to see if the job is really for you.

- **Fill in the blanks.** As you review the description, try to keep in mind the other leadership tasks that were not included. For example, a posting for a chief operations officer may include a wide range of responsibilities, but make no mention of fundraising, public relations, and the like. Do your homework to determine if these tasks are being handled by others or if they will also fall under your jurisdiction.

- **Gauge flexibility options.** Will this position offer budgetary and staffing flexibility in the event of change, such as shifting market trends, new technologies, or other unforeseen demands? This is important to ensure that the leader will not get saddled with unwanted and misplaced tasks. So many added responsibilities seem to evolve over time or to drop mysteriously onto the leader's lap. Flexibility allows leaders to respond to new challenges and demands quickly and properly.

- **Study the bigger picture.** Visit the company's website and learn as much as you can about it. Learn more about their corporate location and structure. Study what they do and where they do it.

Google the company and see what is being reported about it in the media. Read their blog to learn what they are writing about. Visit their social media pages and read their posts and comments. The more that you can learn about the company and its values and practices, the better.

- **Look at the mission statement.** While on the website, see if there is a posted mission statement or some other statement of purpose or values. This will tell you about what the company prides itself in, emphasizes, and views as its unique qualities. These may include transparency, environmental sustainability, superior customer service, or some other values-based mission. As you consider applying, use this knowledge to determine how your values and objectives line up with theirs. Assume that the interviewer will ask you what attracted you to her company. Study up on such information so that you can respond with an educated answer, such as how the company's mission resonates with you and how you can help it advance further.

> *Naturally, there are going to be many aspects of the job that you will only learn over time. The more that you can do to go into the position informed and ready, however, the better you will position yourself for success.*

- **Search your contacts.** See if there is someone in the company that you know that may have some inside information about the position, the organizational culture, and the like. If nobody comes to mind, search your contact lists and professional connections (such as those on LinkedIn) to see who does or did work there. Perhaps you know someone who does business with them or would have other reason to be intimately familiar with the company.

- **Interview the interviewer.** During the interview process, ask as many questions as you can about the job. Include questions about the environment, the culture, and shared values. Be sufficiently open-ended to elicit more than yes/no responses. Then, listen carefully to the adjectives the interviewer(s) use(s). What aspects of working there does she choose to talk about? That can be very telling.

- **Share what you know.** Employers take note of candidates who are well informed about the job responsibilities and the company itself. This demonstrates that you made a deliberate decision to apply for the job after considering the facts, rather than just out of desperation for a job. It also says that you are well studied and well prepared—qualities that employers really like.

- **Get a good look around.** Don't leave before taking a tour of the place. At the least, try to peer into some of the workspaces. You can gain insight into the work environment by studying the layout, the décor, the energy level, dress code, and much more.

Naturally, there are going to be many aspects of the job that you will only learn over time. The more that you can do to go into the position informed and ready, however, the better you will position yourself for success.

CHAPTER 8

Get Your Agreements in Order

In business, the idea of measuring what you are doing,
picking the measurements that count like customer
satisfaction and performance...you thrive on that.

BILL GATES

~

After I had interviewed multiple times for my position of school principal (both over the phone and in person), I knew that a formal offer would be forthcoming. It took some time, however, for the contract to arrive. When it finally did, there was trouble written all over it, in the sense that it was vague and lacked a clear job description. In the end, the contractual negotiation period extended much longer than the original interviewing process and courtship combined.

Once you have a contract in hand, make sure that it clearly details what you are responsible for achieving and the full parameters of the job. A good employment contract will spell out your salary and benefits package, such as health, life or disability insurance, or retirement accounts. Other important items include:

- The term of employment

- Vacation and sick-day policies

- A method for resolving employment-related disputes (such as mediation or arbitration)

- Reasons and grounds for termination

- Noncompete and nondisclosure agreements

The benefits of you doing this will include:

- **Clear, immediate focus.**
A well-written contract will help you focus your energies from day one. While you may need some time to gather information and lay foundations before acting in any meaningful sense (more about that later), you will at least know what is expected of you from the very beginning and the terms under which you are operating.

> *Once you have a contract in hand, make sure that it clearly details what you are responsible for achieving… make sure the contract also clearly details the parameters of your job.*

- **More targeted feedback.** Another benefit is that it will allow for more focused feedback as well as an easier, more accurate, and more useful evaluation process. We will discuss this in greater detail below.

- **Managing expectations.** It will also cover you in case others' expectations of you change over time without your input or consent. This is very important and can often be overlooked. Jobs evolve and change, particularly those in dynamic organizations. As market trends and other factors make their impact, leaders are expected to adjust accordingly. They must, however, be able to have a say in that process, and by putting things in writing, they can better respond to unwelcome or unanticipated demands.

The next step is to come to an agreement on an evaluation process. This involves several components. First, you need to be clear on who is doing the assessing; it may be a direct supervisor, the board of directors, a board subcommittee, or another party. Whoever it is, make sure to meet with them to discuss the evaluation process.

In that discussion, several areas need to be covered. These include frequency of assessment, the assessment tool, and whether there will be a particular set of priorities that will take precedence and carry disproportionate value.

- **Frequency.** Frequent feedback gives leaders the opportunity to make adjustments as needed, well before things go sideways in a serious way. It also allows for modifications of goals if that is required. While each situation may dictate its own feedback frequency, there is no question that a once-annual review is not sufficient.

- **The tool makes all the difference.** What evaluative tool will you be using? Does it offer clear, objective descriptors of job performance and ask for supportive evidence, or does it leave things open for subjective interpretation? The clearer and more detailed it is, the better.

- **Identify the focus.** This point cannot be overstated. It is near impossible for leaders to excel at everything, especially if there is an expectation for them to work on specific personal or organizational goals. Those who are doing the assessing need to be willing to let certain things go if there is to be a fair and accurate process. Make sure that the evaluation tool reflects this by weighting those criteria that matter most, rather than assigning equal value to all professional competencies.

- **And keep it there.** It can be challenging for assessors to remain disciplined in their views when constituents are clamoring for various other gains or complaining about "noncore" areas. It can be even harder for the assessee to keep the group focused on the agreed-to goals. Hopefully, enough equity and trust can be built between parties to allow for redirection to occur without it being taken personally or compromising the outcome.

A leader would also be well-advised to continue to share positive news and achievements with his assessor(s) in a steady but not pushy manner. If there is doubt about how best to proactively share progress, be sure to discuss the desired frequency and delivery method of such information.

Often, prospective leaders fail to go through all or part of this process, either because they are not aware of its benefits or they fear that too much insistence will jeopardize their candidacy. While this is understandable, it is the responsibility of a job seeker to perform due diligence and set himself up for success. If he fails to do so, he may get saddled with tasks and expectations that are onerous, unrealistic, and not what he signed up for.

CHAPTER 9

Learn the Culture

A wise man adapts himself to circumstances,
as water shapes itself to the vessel that contains it.
CHINESE PROVERB

~

About a year or so into my principalship, I attended a leadership seminar together with my board chair. The session was for independent school leaders and board chairs, and focused on matters of governance. While I do not remember the overwhelming majority of the content presented that evening, there was one slide that got my attention. I remember it to this day because it captured a critical leadership concept in one vivid, ominous message.

The slide was entitled, "Hills that heads die on." On the slide was a list of ostensibly insignificant decisions that had been made by different school leaders, such as changing the direction of the carpool line or clearing out older artifacts from the trophy case. To our collective surprise, the presenter shared that this was not a joke. In fact, these were primary contributing factors to actual school leader terminations.

While the concerns that were listed on that slide may have appeared petty to the casual observer, they were important issues to the respective local school populations. The leaders in each case had not taken the time to learn the culture and find out what really mattered to their people before making what they thought to be innocuous, constructive changes. Never would they have imagined losing their jobs over these decisions.

~

During your transition period, you want to learn as much as you can about the existing workplace culture. Take time to study the important traditions, symbols, events, and even behaviors that hold meaning for your people.

Ask lots of questions, but be sure to do so in a way that suggests interest, curiosity, and nonjudgment. Consider introducing questions as follows: "Just curious," "How have we historically," and "Can you help me understand?" Tell people that you are genuinely interested in finding out the insider's view of how the organization works. The answers to these questions will help you to avoid pitfalls.

Possible questions follow.

CORE BELIEFS AND VALUES

- Does the company have a stated set of cultural values?
- Are the values stable, widely communicated, and continuously emphasized?
- How is success defined and celebrated?
- What qualities are rewarded?
- What sacred cows do I need to be aware of?
- What stories do people tell here?

HEROES AND HURDLES

- Who are the organizational heroes and heroines, and what did they do to achieve such status?
- Were there any crises that needed to be overcome? How were they handled?
- What were the milestone events in the organization's history?
- How has management reacted to blunders and mistakes?
- How have firings and layoffs been handled?

WORKPLACE CONDITIONS

- What's it really like to work here?
- How do employees and customers expect to be treated?
- What do you like most about working here?
- What do you like least about working here?
- What anecdotes are told about senior management?

WORK ENVIRONMENT

- What objects, artifacts, and other physical signs are in the workplace?
- What do people place on their desks?
- What hangs on the walls?
- How is office space (offices, cubicles, common areas) allocated?

EMPLOYEE INTERACTIONS

- Do people work independently or collaboratively?
- Do people interact with others at all levels of the organization, or primarily with their manager and peers?
- Are there any silos or warring factions?

BEHAVIORS

- What behaviors and attitudes are expected?
- How are such behaviors reinforced and rewarded?
- What is the biggest mistake one could make?

COMMUNICATION PRACTICES

- How are coworkers expected to communicate with each other?
- What is the preferred means of communication: e-mail, telephone, chat, or in person?
- Is the style of written communication (memos and e-mail messages) formal or informal?
- Are messages usually brief or detailed?
- Who is copied on the communications: numerous people or only people directly involved?
- What is the extent of transparency in sharing information and making decisions?

DECISION-MAKING

- How are decisions made and problems solved?
- Who needs to be included in the decision-making process?
- Are employees empowered to make decisions independently?

MEETINGS

- How often are meetings held?
- Who attends?
- How are they conducted: formally with set agendas or informally?
- Do meetings serve primarily to share information, or to discuss, learn, and problem-solve?

TRAINING AND ONBOARDING

- What training and onboarding processes are in place?
- Is this a learning and teaching workplace?

BEYOND THE WORKPLACE

- Do people socialize during lunch breaks and after hours?
- Does the organization organize social events?
- Is there an expectation of attendance at such events?

Perhaps you can identify one or more official chroniclers who have been around for a while and possess a balanced, informed view of the organization's history and cultural development. Such people can be a tremendous resource as you seek to understand existing mindsets and behaviors. They can also offer perspective when you are ready to consider new ideas and want to get safe feedback.

Once you better understand the culture, seek to embrace it and become part of it, even if it feels a bit awkward at times. One of the hardest cultural components for me during my tenure as head of school was morning lineup. My predecessor had a unique routine that he used for years to get things started. It had become part of the school fabric and everyone—students, teachers, and parents—knew it by heart. For me, the practice was strange and awkward, but I knew better than to try to mess with it. For my entire time at the school, I followed that time-honored tradition exactly as I had inherited it, and did the best that I could to roll with it every day, with maximal energy and engagement. I even added a few of my own wrinkles in, which nobody seemed to mind.

Of course, the role of the leader is to help continue to mold and shape the culture. Over time, it may come to look very different than the culture that you inherited. We will talk about how to drive such changes in a later chapter. Still, your short-term goal in most cases is to familiarize yourself with the existing culture and not step on any time bombs as you get acclimated. By working to kick things off positively, you will greatly increase your likelihood of gaining colleagues' trust and support from the outset. This will hold you in good stead as you become better acquainted and establish yourself in your new role.

CHAPTER 10

Know Whom You're Following

One of the things we often miss in succession planning
is that it should be gradual and thoughtful, with lots of
sharing of information and knowledge and perspective, so
that it's almost a nonevent when it happens.

ANNE M. MULCAHY

∽

A leadership transition is one of the most important, yet underestimated aspects of a new leader's experience. It helps to frame his role and the relationship that he develops with his team. If managed well, such transitions can make all the difference in promoting acceptance from within the ranks, and allow you, the new leader, the time and patience necessary to get acclimated and begin to build equity.

Following the 2007 baseball season, New York Yankees manager Joe Torre found himself in an uncomfortable situation. His team had once again been unceremoniously ousted from the playoffs, this time in the division round by Cleveland. In the off-season, Torre received a tepid vote of confidence from team management which came in the form of a one-year contract extension offer.

Torre decided that the time was right to move on (he would later head off to Los Angeles to manage the Dodgers.) The leading candidates to replace him were Joe Girardi and Don Mattingly, Torre's disciples (as Yankees coaches) and former Yankees players (Girardi had played under Torre; Mattingly, a Yankee hero, had retired shortly before Torre was hired.) Eventually, it was Girardi who was selected to replace his former boss and mentor.

Obviously, replacing Torre was no simple task for the junior Joe. Although he had fallen off a bit in recent years (the Yankees had not been to the World

Series since 2003 and had not won since 2000), Joe Torre was still a New York star—someone who had brought the Yankees back to earlier levels of greatness following years of failed expectations and instability under former owner George Steinbrenner. He was a born-and-bred New Yorker and a real class act. Add to the mix that Girardi had been hired instead of the great Mattingly, and you can just imagine the pressure that he was facing during his first Spring Training in 2008. In the words of General Manager Brian Cashman, "Anybody trying to follow that, it's an impossible job. So I think the transition was tough for Joe Girardi to establish who he was in the shadow of Joe Torre."[14]

How did Girardi manage to make it in New York City under such conditions? Specifically, how did he survive Year One (2008), which turned out to be the first year since the strike-shortened 1994 season in which the Yankees failed to qualify for post-season baseball?

Surely, there were many factors that helped Girardi get through the transition period, including coming back to win the 2009 championship. But the current skipper also credits the man whom he followed. In reflecting on that experience with MLB.com reporter Barry Bloom, Girardi spoke about his approach as well as the support that he received from Torre. "I think any manager that you follow, it's important that you do it your own way," Girardi said. "That was the first thing Joe told me. But obviously there was a ton of success here and there was an expectation here. It was important to me to carry on that success and expectation. In that way, it was a little bit difficult. But Joe made it easier because of some of the discussions that we had."[15]

> *Seek to learn about the special relationships and other interpersonal nuances. Find out whatever you can about past challenges and successes, as well as the cultural components that define the organization and the way that people relate to it.*

Naturally, each transition process is different. An outgoing leader may

[14] Bloom, Barry M. "Barry M. Bloom: Following Joe Torre, Manager Joe Girardi Able to Also Succeed with Yankees." Major League Baseball. February 18, 2014. Accessed February 22, 2017. http://m.mlb.com/news/article/67892380/barry-m-bloom-following-joe-torre-manager-joe-girardi-able-to-also-succeed-with-yankees/.

[15] Ibid.

not always be so supportive of his successor, such as when there was no preexisting relationship between them, or if the circumstances of departure did not foster a giving spirit. In my case, my predecessor did not even finish out the year, as he traveled with his ailing wife to Israel to live out her final days there. Communication at that time between us was naturally limited. Still, incoming leaders would be wise to do whatever they can to gain insight and support from the person they will be succeeding.

Speak to the departing executive about the company's history and key players. Seek to learn about the special relationships and other interpersonal nuances. Find out whatever you can about past challenges and successes, as well as the cultural components that define the organization and the way that people relate to it. An outgoing leader can be a treasure trove of information and often really wants to be able to help and share. Moreover, by demonstrating interest, the new leader shows that he respects the efforts of those who brought the organization to its present level of success.

At the same time, be sure to learn about and then not repeat past mistakes. Besides speaking with the old boss, you should also talk with staffers. You will almost certainly hear about past practices or policies that they would like to see changed. Of course, any talk about how things have been should be done carefully and with great respect. Whether your predecessor is leaving of his or her own volition or was shown the door, you will speak volumes about your own leadership style and character by taking pains to avoid slighting him or her.

CHAPTER 11

Find a Good Mentor

If you cannot see where you are going,
ask someone who has been there before.

J LOREN NORRIS

~

A recent study looked at a select group of top-performing New York City based tech companies.[16] The short list included *Huffington Post*, Shutterstock, and Tumblr. The researchers found that many of the entrepreneurs leading successful start-ups had strong personal connections to the founders of other winning companies. One of the most powerful connections identified in their analysis was the benefit of mentoring relationships, which gave younger leaders the opportunity to learn from their older, more experienced peers.

~

When I began as a head-of-school, I got in touch with someone who helped to arrange mentors for new principals. After a short while, I was assigned an experienced mentor from a school on the other side of the country. He agreed to help me as a favor, and, for a while, we met once weekly on the phone and discussed many of the challenges and specifics of my new job.

I found those conversations useful in terms of getting some meaningful advice and guidance from a seasoned pro. I also was comforted to learn that many of my challenges were commonplace and shared by a large percentage of my colleagues. Predictably, as the school year progressed and his schedule became increasingly more filled, our time together dwindled to the point that the relationship had practically ended on its own. At that point, I felt like I had no one that I could turn to in order to unburden myself and get counsel.

---

[16] Morris, Rhett. "Mentors Are The Secret Weapons Of Successful Startups." *TechCrunch*. Accessed February 22, 2017. https://techcrunch.com/2015/03/22/mentors-are-the-secret-weapons-of-successful-startups/

One of the most important things for new leaders to do early on (before they start in their new posts, if possible) is to get a mentor. A mentor is someone who can draw from their experience and know-how to offer meaningful advice and direction to others.

Why is a good mentor so important? For starters, mentors help others find their way. No matter how many leadership books you read or blogs you subscribe to, there's a dynamic element to leadership that no text can fully describe or account for. The right mentors have been there, done that, and can use their experiences to offer direction and clarity. For many new leaders, their positions feel like a journey through a corn maze in which it's often difficult (if not impossible) to navigate from their ground-level perspective. A good mentor can position himself above the tall brush, as it were, and point the mentee in the right direction.

Mentors come in all shapes and sizes. Sometimes, you can find a mentor within your new organization; ideally, someone who has already done what you're now doing. By knowing the company well, the mentor can help you more quickly understand the new culture and its practices as you adjust to your new responsibilities and environment. He or she can help you translate terms and policies unique to your new office while helping you steer clear of potential landmines and other obstacles.

For some people, like a new CEO, it may be easier to look elsewhere for an individual who has the requisite experience and can keep concerns and insecurities confidential. In such cases, it may behoove a new leader to find multiple mentors, each one offering something unique and meaningful to help them grow. Be careful, though, to avoid the "too many cooks" or "too many batting coaches" syndrome, which can lead to mixed messages, confusion, and ultimately paralysis by analysis.

Regardless of how many mentors you choose to connect with, it's most important to find the right kind of person to confide in and seek guidance from. The following list of strategies can help you pair up properly.

- **Focus on the person, not the position.** Often, we seek mentors who did and/or do exactly what we are looking to achieve. While that makes sense, you may sometimes have to choose between the person and the position that they hold. According to Indra Nooyi, the CEO of PepsiCo, such mentors could be anyone. "If I hadn't had mentors, I wouldn't be here today," she said. "I'm a product of great mentoring, great coaching...Coaches or mentors are very important. They could be anyone—your husband, other family members, or your boss."[17]

> *Mentors help others find their way. No matter how many leadership books you read or blogs you subscribe to, there's a dynamic element to leadership that no text can fully describe or account for.*

- **Find the right person for the need, not the relationship.** In a similar sense, a mentoring relationship is more about the mentoring and less about the actual relationship. While the relationship is certainly important and will motivate you to want to get together with your mentor and hear what he or she has to say, the actual substance of his or her words is most critical, not the pleasant time spent over coffee.

- **Be flexible about where and how you meet.** An early morning coffee at Starbucks may be your preference, but that's not always going to work, especially if you and your mentor work in different places. Again, the key thing is the *who*. Make the *where* and *how* revolve around what works best for the mentor.

- **Is he or she a good storyteller?** Mentorship can often be about advice, but it need not be. Sometimes, the mentor will not have all of the answers that you need. Maybe what you need isn't answers anyway, but a direction. A mentor who owns a deep set of experiences and can use those to tell rich, meaningful, and relevant stories can often do you more good than one who thinks that they have *the* solution to every problem.

---

[17] Walker, Keith, and Bob Bayles. *Reflections on Facilitating Learning in Prairie Spirit*. Saskatoon: Turning Point Global, 2016: 53.

CHAPTER 12

Become Aware of Your Blind Spots

Honest feedback is hard to take, especially from a relative, a friend, an acquaintance or a stranger.

FRANKLIN P. JONES

~

I once found myself in search of new employment. The situation that I was leaving had been complex, to say the least, and I worried that perceptions of failure would dog me as I sought new opportunities.

As part of the interview process, I met with an organization's chief executive, who would have been my new direct supervisor. After interviewing in person, he took the time to try to research my situation to determine whether I would be an asset to him. Soon after our meeting, he called me to say that he had spoken with people who were familiar with my performance and was prepared to hire me now that he better understood my "blind spots."

As you could likely imagine, this half-baked endorsement did not do much to increase my desire to work for him. On a positive note, the conversation did alert me to an important aspect of leadership that leaders often fail to perceive: namely, their blind spots.

John C. Maxwell defines a blind spot as "an area in the lives of people in which they *continually* do not see themselves or their situation realistically." Leadership blind spots can be found in many areas, such as workplace knowledge or expertise, leadership style, relationships, or some other key domain.

A Hay Group study shows that the senior leaders in an organization are more likely to overrate themselves and to develop blind spots that can hinder their effectiveness as leaders.[18] Another study by Development Dimensions International Inc. found that 89 percent of front-line leaders have at least one blind spot in their leadership skills.[19]

Let's be frank. We all have them, regardless of our robust talents and successes. We may know a lot about our work and our industry and think that there's nothing else for use to learn. Perhaps we see ourselves as connecting effectively with others and fail to identify problematic relations. Maybe we think that we run great meetings, while participants feel disengaged or that we do not solicit sufficient input. Regardless of the issue, we need to be cognizant that things aren't always as rosy as we may think, and it would behoove us to gain and maintain as clear a picture a possible about our job performance.

According to Robert Bruce Shaw, there are a few particular blind spots that many leaders suffer from. These include:[20]

- **Strategic thinking.** Shaw maintains that many leaders are better at managing operations than they are at thinking strategically. Leaders who overestimate their strategic capabilities can face serious problems when they're promoted into more senior-level roles. Such roles put a premium on identifying and acting on new growth opportunities, which is something that's hard to focus on if you're bogged down in managerial tasks.

- **All-knowingness.** Some bosses think that they know more than everybody else about everything and anything. Executives in this category don't consider others' points of view on most issues. They often prefer being right to being effective. Not only are they not always correct, but they distance themselves from their brain trust and make it harder to explore challenges and potential pitfalls.

- **Assumption.** Many executives make the mistake of assuming that other people are just like them. They figure that others are motivated by similar things, think in the same way, and would natu-

---

[18] "Executive Blind Spots." Hay Group RSS. Accessed February 22, 2017. http://www.haygroup.com/us/downloads/details.aspx?id=7347.

[19] "Finding the First Rung." DDI International. Accessed February 22, 2017. http://www.ddiworld.com/resources/library/trend-research/finding-the-first-rung.

[20] Shaw, Robert B. *Leadership Blindspots: How Successful Leaders Identify and Overcome the Weaknesses That Matter.* Wiley, 2014.

rally agree with the leader's decisions. As preposterous as this may sound, many leaders simply think that others see things just as they do. Shaw said that this false assumption could lead to poor decisions and weak work relationships. Sometimes leaders exacerbate this problem by hiring people who are like them instead of hiring indi-

> *Regardless of the issue, we need to be cognizant that things aren't always as rosy as we may think, and it would behoove us to gain and maintain as clear a picture a possible about our job performance.*

viduals who have complementary skills. In a talk titled "The Top Ten Mistakes of Entrepreneurs," Guy Kawasaki includes one of the most pervasive blind spots that leaders often have. As Kawasaki puts it, "You need to balance off all the talents in a company."[21]

- **Stuck-in-the-past blindness.** Often, leaders assume that their past experiences can help them fix new problems. While this may be true at times, Shaw says that leaders will often default to old methods that do not fit the current situation. Larry Stephens once said, "If the only tool you have is a hammer, you tend to see every problem as a nail." Often, leaders' desire to take action hinders their ability to pursue or consider alternative responses.

So how can leaders see past their blind spots to ensure that they are not misled about their performance and, more importantly, fail to provide the kind of objective, supportive and collaborative leadership that their people want? Shaw suggests these strategies:

- **Install a warning system.** Have at least one person who can offer you regular feedback that prevents you from being blindsided. I did this as a head of school (we called it a Head Support Committee), and that worked wonders for me in terms of getting genuine, constructive feedback in a way that did not make members feel uncomfortable in sharing their thoughts.

---

[21] *The Top 10 Mistakes of Entrepreneurs.* Produced by Berkeley-Haas. Performed by Guy Kawasaki. March 7, 2013. Accessed February 22, 2017. https://youtu.be/HHjgK6p4nrw.

- **Build a good team.** Build a diverse team of smart people who are willing to engage with the leader and each other in productive talks and debates on the best path forward.

- **Assess yourself from time to time.** Use 360-degree feedback, skip-level interviews, or similar feedback mechanisms that point out areas of potential weakness.[22, 23] We will discuss this in greater detail below.

Here are some other ideas worth considering:

- **Be reflective.** Leaders would do well to think back on their past successes and failures as a leader. What has worked for you until now? Where did you get yourself into trouble?

- **Work on relationships.** Relationships are the glue that holds everything in the workplace together. So much of what drives success and failure can be traced to the nature of the relational dynamic. Leaders would be well advised to work hard on building and maintaining relationships.

Keep in mind that most folks don't expect perfection from their leaders. They do, however, want their leaders to be self-aware and take proper steps to minimize the impact of their blind spots. While these strategies may not eliminate all of our deficiencies, they can certainly reduce the frequency of them appearing while also diminishing their impact.

---

[22] 360-degree feedback is a system or process in which employees receive confidential, anonymous feedback from the people who work around them, typically including the employee's manager, peers, and direct reports.

[23] A skip-level interview is a discussion facilitated by a senior level manager with an employee, or group of employees, within the same business group.

SECTION 3

START SMART

CHAPTER 13

Get off on the Right Foot

Joining a new company is akin to an organ transplant—and you're the new organ. If you're not thoughtful in adapting to the new situation, you could end up being attacked by the organizational immune system and rejected.

MICHAEL D. WATKINS

∼

In a 2009 article, *U.S. News and World* Report writer Ken Walsh described the first 100 days of Franklin D. Roosevelt's presidential tenure.[24] In that short period, Roosevelt pushed an incredible fifteen major bills through Congress, such as the Glass-Steagall Act and Federal Deposit Insurance Corp. "Faced with the spreading catastrophe of the Depression in 1933," wrote Walsh, "Franklin D. Roosevelt knew from the start that what Americans wanted most of all was reassurance that under his leadership, they could weather the storm…This began an unprecedented period of experimentation during which Roosevelt tried different methods to ease the Depression…His success in winning congressional approval became the stuff of legend…The new president immediately established a new, infectious atmosphere of optimism."

For the past eight decades since FDR's whirlwind initiation, the first 100 days of a president's tenure in office has been used as a benchmark to measure productivity and effectiveness. Congressional leaders and political pundits closely study the new leader's behaviors and agenda items during this early period to see what type of leadership they can expect for the balance of the term and possibly beyond.

---

[24] Ken Walsh. "The First 100 Days: Franklin Roosevelt Pioneered the 100-Day Concept." *US News &World Report*, February 12, 2009.
http://www.usnews.com/news/history/articles/2009/02/12/the-first-100-days-franklin-roosevelt-pioneered-the-100-day-concept

A similar dynamic exists with new business and organizational leaders, though for them the period is usually a bit shorter, at ninety days. Ninety days is equivalent to a business quarter, which is a meaningful timeframe in the professional world. Companies often track how they're doing based on how much progress they make each quarter, and that includes a leader's performance. While the nonprofit world may not use this metric, a three-month timeframe has still become accepted as a legitimate barometer for measuring new leader effectiveness.

New leaders may feel an overwhelming sense of pressure to succeed immediately in their new position. Superiors often expect the new leader to correct an existing problem within the department, such as low productivity. Performing under such pressure is often challenging for new leaders.

Leaders' early actions, especially for those with more demanding leadership responsibilities, can often determine whether they will ultimately succeed or fail. Harvard professor and leadership transition expert Michael Watkins writes in his best-selling book, *The First 90 Days*, "When leaders derail, their problems can almost always be traced to vicious cycles that developed in the first few months on the job."[25] According to Watkins, what leaders do early on during a job transition is what matters most. Colleagues and others form opinions about them based on the limited information that they have available, and, once those opinions are formed, it can be quite difficult to change their minds in the months and even years that follow.

Leaders that make positive first impressions by doing such things as demonstrating a willingness to listen, to share leadership, and to be decisive, will typically be given the benefit of the doubt when relationships derail or decision-making comes under question. Early mistakes, on the other hand, will often lead people to draw negative conclusions about the new leader's capacity to improve things and will cause them to become cynical and impatient.

"Transitions are times when momentum builds, or it doesn't, when opinions about new leaders begin to crystallize," Watkins wrote. "It's a time when feedback loops—virtuous cycles or vicious ones—get established. Significant missteps feed downward spirals that can be hard to arrest. So,

---

[25] Watkins, Michael. *The First 90 Days: Critical Success Strategies for New Leaders at All Levels.* Boston, MA: Harvard Business School Press, 2003.

it's far better for new leaders to get off to a good start by building personal credibility and political capital, rather than dig themselves into holes and have to clamber back out."

These four strategies can be particularly helpful during this critical time:

- **Achieve organizational alignment.** Ensure that the organization's existing structure can support the chosen strategy and that it has the systems and skills to realize your strategic vision.

- **Build your team.** Once your vision is intact, evaluate, choose and/or restructure your leadership team and organization to ensure that you are well-positioned going forward.

- **Expedite everyone.** Help everyone around you quickly make the necessary transitions to optimize their performances and support you in your journey.

- **Create coalitions.** Build working alliances with key people outside your line of reporting who can help you achieve your goals.

There is one exception to the above formula for new leader success: turnaround situations. While positive impressions are always important for new leaders, during a turnaround situation, they take a back seat to results. The emphasis at this time must be placed on action and outcomes—the kinds of things that lead to immediate improvements. For example, if one of your products or divisions is struggling, decide as quickly as possible if you should either kill it or devote more resources to it and pump up sales.

> *Be sure to maintain a long-time view as well. Remind your people regularly that this is just the beginning of a long process that, with their help, can produce tremendous results for everyone.*

Turnaround situations usually offer leaders their best opportunity to make an impact because of the existing mandate and appetite for change. As much as your people want to connect with you and become more secure in their relationships with the new boss, they are most interested in results that will enhance their general work environment and improve the bottom line.

Finally, as much as we can appreciate the importance of the transition period and the many opportunities that it may offer, we must be sure to maintain a long-time view as well. Remind your people regularly that this is just the beginning of a long process that, with their help, can produce tremendous results for everyone. In the words of John Fitzgerald Kennedy: "All this will not be finished in the first hundred days. Nor will it be finished in the first thousand days, nor in the life of this administration, nor even perhaps in our lifetime on this planet. But let us begin."

CHAPTER 14

Make a Great First Impression

*Because you never get a second chance
to make a first impression.*

HEAD & SHOULDERS DANDRUFF SHAMPOO
COMMERCIAL, C. 1990.

~

One rainy day during the Revolutionary War, George Washington rode up to a group of soldiers attempting to raise a wooden beam to a high position. The corporal in charge was shouting encouragement, but the soldiers still couldn't position it correctly. General Washington asked the corporal why he didn't join in and help, to which the corporal replied, "Don't you realize that I am the corporal?"

Very politely, Washington replied, "I beg your pardon, Mr. Corporal, I did." Washington dismounted his horse and went to work with the soldiers to get the oak beam in position. As they finished, Washington said, "If you should need help again, call on Washington, your commander-in-chief, and I will come."[26]

Imagine the first impression that Washington made on those men. Any doubt whether these soldiers gave their all on the battlefield for their commander-in-chief?

We all recognize the importance of first impressions. It is during the first few moments of interaction that we begin to size up others in our attempt to determine who that person is, the qualities that they possess, and how they operate. While this is the case for all people that we meet, it is particularly true for new leaders. Employees are often extremely anxious to become acquainted with the new boss and determine how they will get along. Even

---

[26] Maxwell, John C. *The Five Levels of Leadership: Proven Steps to Maximize Your Potential.* New York: Center Street, 2011.

bosses who have been promoted from within are being watched carefully for signs of leadership style and intentions.

While you can't stop people from making snap decisions about you, you can make those decisions work in your favor. One thing to keep in mind is that first impressions are more heavily influenced by nonverbal cues than by verbal ones. Research also teaches us that such impressions are made in just a handful of seconds, so the first interaction is really important.

Here are some ideas to help make a positive first impression:

- **Breathe deep and relax.** Some people are naturals when it comes to meeting new people. Others are not. In fact, new situations can often invoke strong feelings of anxiety, particularly for those who are not used to being at the center of attention. If that's you, consider using breathing and relaxing techniques such as centering to help you release tension and put yourself at ease.[27]

- **Envision the situation in advance.** One of the most commonly taught practices for public speakers and performers is to envision the crowd in advance. This helps foster a sense of familiarity, which allows you just to be yourself when it matters most.

- **Project a great attitude.** Attitude comes across right away. Before you get in front of people, make a conscious choice about the kind of attitude you want to project. Think of it as a great opportunity to quickly make a bunch of new fans.

- **Offer a firm handshake.** Shaking hands helps establish quick rapport. Doing so firmly lets people know that you are confident, self-assured, and excited to meet them.

- **Smile warmly.** A smile says, "I'm friendly, caring and approachable." It also says, "I like you and am glad to see you."

- **Ask for (and learn) their names.** Dale Carnegie famously wrote in *How to Win Friends and Influence People* that "names are the sweetest and most important sound in any language." People love when you use their name, and you can score serious points by learning their names quickly.

---

[27] To learn more about centering visit https://www.mindtools.com/pages/article/newTCS_83.htm

- **Be a good conversationalist.** Be talkative and get to know people. Ask about their background and position and let them know that you look forward to working with them. And don't forget to listen actively, with a posture that says, "I care about what you are telling me." As Dale Carnegie said, a person can make more friends in two months by becoming interested in other people than she can in two years by trying to get other people interested in her.

Of course, these strategies should be front-and-center any time that you seek to impress. Carnegie wrote of a certain Robert Cryer, who was the manager of a computer department for a midsized company. Cryer was desperately trying to recruit a Ph.D. in computer science. The one that he hired had also been pursued by some larger, better-known companies. Sometime after the young man accepted Cryer's offer, he told his new boss that the energy and positivity that he used to recruit him had been the main difference-maker in his decision. "Your voice sounded as if you were glad to hear from me—that you really wanted me to be part of your organization."

> *While you can't stop people from making snap decisions about you, you can make those decisions work in your favor. One thing to keep in mind is that first impressions are more heavily influenced by nonverbal cues than by verbal ones.*

CHAPTER 15

Quell the Fear Factor

The oldest and strongest emotion of mankind is fear, and the oldest and strongest kind of fear is fear of the unknown.

H. P. LOVECRAFT

~

A handful of community leaders approached me about halfway through my first year as a school leader. Some teachers—particularly the tenured vets—were concerned with certain aspects of my leadership style and were starting to vent to board members and other people of influence. After hearing these people out, I asked them what most people in a similar situation would want to know. "Why aren't they coming to me with this?" I was told that they were afraid of losing their jobs.

To be honest, I found their response hard to accept. I knew that not everything had gone smoothly over the first few months on the job (there was *so* much to learn and understand!) and I also wasn't the one to whom they offered their allegiances (I had not hired and then rehired them year over year). Still, I certainly did not think of myself as scary or a sworn and committed change agent, at least not on the personnel level. But then something happened that changed my entire perspective.

Soon after those conversations, I invited two veteran teachers to my office. My goal was to better understand the faculty's concerns and what I could do to address them. These two women had both been on staff for years and were well-connected and respected internally. I felt that they were likely to have valuable information and insights to share.

As I sat across the table from them and explained my intentions, they looked at me studiously. When I finished, both exhaled deeply, and one even laughed that uncomfortable kind of laugh that we use when we are released from a subdued fear. When I asked for clarification, I was told straight out that they had feared the worst for themselves before entering my office. My words had helped put them at ease.

Why were they fearful? The primary gist of it was that I was too distant. I spent too much time in my office and did not take enough time to ask questions and share what I was thinking. They knew that I had been hired to make some changes and had already done so, though on a small scale. The absence of any assurances led them to worry about their job security.

Research tells us that when presented side-by-side, fear will always trump opportunity. It is that powerful. Routine and predictability give us a sense of control. When there are big changes, we are suddenly thrown into a state of uncertainty. "What am I doing wrong," we ask ourselves, "to make my employer think that things should change?"

New management in particular sets off a lot of different anxieties. Employees wonder how their relationship will be with the new boss and how he will approve of their work. They fret over whether they will remain as valued members of the team and begin to worry about a possible new role. Especially in our fluid, twenty-first century work environment that continues to evolve and tends not to offer the predictable, lifer positions that many baby boomers and their parents enjoyed, a new boss needs to be aware of such anxieties and take proactive steps to quell them.

This is particularly true when a newly promoted leader is asked to manage and lead employees who were once his peers. The sudden change in the relationship often causes confusion and discomfort for both employees and the new leader. Employees may also feel resentment towards the new leader for being promoted instead of them.

Of course, this is not to say that every holdover will have a place in your new landscape. You may have been brought in to make changes and to evaluate the old guard. Regardless, new leaders can take these steps to ease tensions and offer their new coworkers more peace of mind.

- **Make a great first impression.** As noted above, when you meet your team, let them know that you're excited to work with them and support their efforts.

- **Be a great listener.** Learn to listen well. When people can speak freely with you and believe that you are genuinely interested in what they have to say, they will come to trust you more and worry less.

- **Communicate effectively.** Use personal, direct conversation and in-person meetings wherever possible to share your thoughts and ideas. By adding the nonverbal components of communication, we more effectively convey intent, trustworthiness, and reliability. Leaders who are great storytellers are also better able to gain staff support and compliance.

> *Research tells us that when presented side-by-side, fear will always trump opportunity. It is that powerful.*

- **Build strong relationships**. Listening and communication are two building blocks in helping you to build relationships. Once you have succeeded in developing positive professional relationships, it is more likely that people within the organization will candidly update you on internal developments, warn you about potential challenges or land mines, and even tolerate your mistakes more willingly. This can be very valuable, particularly at the beginning of your tenure.

In taking these steps, leaders demonstrate a genuine interest in and respect for their people and their new environment. While this may not fully assuage the fears of those who worry about their new boss and her agenda, it should help put the majority of folks at ease as they settle into their new reality.

CHAPTER 16

How to Gain More Experience in Less Time

Mistakes are the usual bridge between inexperience and wisdom.

PHYLLIS GRISSIM-THEROUX

～

We all recognize the importance of job and life experience, especially for leaders. Experience gives leaders context for important decisions they must make and insight into how best to lead, motivate, and respond to their people. Experienced leaders have been through the wringer before and can use their past learning and decisions to guide them moving forward.

Inexperienced leaders, by contrast, are likelier to fall into traps that can cost them in the short- and long-term. Common dangers of inexperienced leaders include: needing to be liked, a propensity towards blaming others for mistakes and failures, emotional and/or impulsive decision-making (and for some, indecisiveness), addressing symptoms rather than root causes, meddling and micromanaging, trying too hard, thinking short-term rather than long-term, and neglecting to credit and express appreciation to those who deserve it.

To reduce the possibility of making such mistakes, new and aspiring leaders should do what they can to gain the benefits of experience before they can get more on-the-job learning under their belts. Consider these strategies to lessen the on-the-job learning curve.

- **Go for training.** Identify educational programs that are reputable, respected, and, more importantly, offer cutting-edge instruction and hands-on learning that translates well into real-life situations.

- **Volunteer.** See if volunteer opportunities exist for such things as managing a project for an overworked leader. If they presently don't, go ahead and pitch an idea. Someone is bound to take you up on it if she thinks you can help. Use the opportunity to engage in meaningful work as well as reflective conversations about the leadership task. In this way, you can learn much about leadership and how to plan for it in a low stakes

Confucius once said, "By three methods we may learn wisdom: first, by reflection, which is noblest; second, by imitation, which is easiest; and third by experience, which is the bitterest."

environment where there is less pressure to perform and a reduced risk of backlash.

- **Find a mentor/peer group.** We noted above how mentors can cut down the learning curve significantly by offering their experiences and sharing their views on how they would handle certain situations. Peer groups for young leaders can fill a similar role and offer the benefit of helping people learn and grow together. These groups also help new leaders build social networks that can be immensely valuable over time.

- **Read/watch leadership experts.** There is much to be gained by reading and/or watching thought leaders discuss their craft and their experiences. Video is simple to access nowadays and can help you accelerate your leadership learning curve. Many leadership and self-help experts recommend reading for at least thirty minutes a day to stay current and deepen your skill set and understanding of important issues.

- **Reflect and take notes.** As you engage in your leadership tasks, take the time to think and reflect. What worked well today and what didn't? What might have happened had you responded differently to that situation or taken more time to learn about the issue before acting? Sometimes we are inclined to try to put failures out of our memories and focus on moving forward. While that may be useful at times, we must be willing to learn from our experiences if we are to avoid making the same mistakes again.

- **Ask for feedback.** Feedback is critical for the reflective process. Ken Blanchard calls it "the breakfast of champions." We may have one perspective on things, but we can be almost assured that at least *some* others see things differently. Work hard to solicit input and be welcoming of others' ideas.

- **Ask lots of questions.** Use questions to keep yourself reflecting often on your leadership practice. Some great ones include:

  — What type of environment am I building around me?

  — How many questions did I ask today?

  — Am I acting or reacting?

  — How am I leveraging everyone's strengths?

  — Whom do I feel threatened by? Why?

  An important component here is to be courageous enough to ask dumb questions. We all want to look smart and give off the impression that we know everything (after all, we don't want them to think that they hired the wrong person). But we have to willingly admit when we don't know something and ask about it if we are to learn and grow. The Talmud (Avot 2:5) teaches, "the bashful student cannot learn." By extension, a bashful (or perhaps prideful) leader cannot learn if they are unwilling to ask.

- **Put yourself in their shoes.** Not too long ago, you were among the led, rather than the one doing the leading. You surely formed many opinions about your leaders and may have even promised yourself that you would never repeat some of their behaviors or decision-making practices when you were given the opportunity. While leadership responsibilities often require you to take on a different perspective, you should still be mindful of how your behaviors or decisions will be received.

Confucius once said, "By three methods we may learn wisdom: first, by reflection, which is noblest; second, by imitation, which is easiest; and third by experience, which is the bitterest." Every new leader would be wise to take the necessary steps to gain as much wisdom as possible without having to endure the bitterness of difficult experiences. By taking time to learn and reflect, as well as to imitate others' (mentors) actions, we can avoid some of the challenges that come through trial and error.

Of course, none of this is to suggest that we must sit back and remain inactive until we can collect meaningful experience. Businessman and *Shark Tank* personality Robert Herjavec has argued, "The best way to get past doubt and inexperience is simply action." Besides, a leader must lead from day one and is often not afforded the luxury of an easy honeymoon transition. Still, the more we can do to compensate for our inexperience with learning and wisdom, the likelier we are to take calculated action and avoid serious error.

CHAPTER 17

Own Your Board

A CEO is a board of directors personified.

MOKOKOMA MOKHONOANA

~

At the end of my first year as a school leader, I met up for breakfast with someone who was very committed to developing school leadership talent and had been instrumental in cultivating a university graduate program in educational administration that I had attended. He had also been a board chair for multiple area schools, including one at which I had taught. I had asked to meet with him so that I could let him enjoy the fruits of his labor (his graduate program had helped me secure my leadership position) while also gleaning from his wisdom and experience as I planned for Year Two.

We talked about the various challenges and successes of the previous year. At one point the topic shifted to the school board. It was then that he looked me straight in the eye and emphatically said, "You need to own your board." By that, he meant that I needed to develop them and their thinking in a way that would position them squarely behind me to advance my agenda. As the CEO, he said, my board could be one of my greatest allies. Conversely, and just as easily, they were positioned to be a significant contributor to my undoing, resulting in an early and unnecessary demise.

He also suggested that I begin the process of developing personal connections with as many individual board members as possible. That included get-to-know-you meetings at the local coffee house. But it also included something deeper, such as establishing a learning partnership with key board members. (In our Orthodox Jewish community, that meant studying Torah together. In other settings, it may center around a different topic of common interest.) I took his advice to heart and set up a weekly study arrangement with two members of the board's executive committee. That relationship allowed for a deeper relationship and increased trust.

~

It goes without saying that the chief executive must make board relations a top priority. While board function and impact range significantly between companies and organizations, it is the board's responsibility, at a minimum, to evaluate you and your work in advancing the organization. (They are also typically tasked with fiduciary oversight and maintenance of the mission.) As with any evaluative process, you want to position yourself on the right side of things, interpersonally and in terms of establishing an agreed-to and properly supported agenda.

Why do so many CEOs hesitate when it comes to attempting to coalesce with their board? Often it has to do with arrogance, naiveté, or some combination thereof. Some leaders often just ignore the board as if they don't even exist until they see a board meeting scheduled or are called to address a problem. They feel that they don't need the board and don't want to be given orders. Others simply assume that if they do their jobs diligently, then everything will be fine. Still others see their boards as a nuisance they must tolerate or, worse, as a bunch of micromanagers who seek to do their jobs for them.

But such thinking is misguided. For the most part, board members sign up because they want to make a difference. They also have egos and want to have a voice and an understanding of how things are functioning. Why create an informational and a relational vacuum that may come to be filled with misinformation and mistrust?

Moreover, your board can be a huge strategic asset. Not only do you want to win them over to your way of thinking and make them confident in your work, but you also want to be able to tap into their collective wisdom for insights and guidance. Remember, these are successful people who likely have much experience to share. Why not take full advantage of that golden opportunity?

There are a few other ways that new leaders can ingratiate themselves with key board members and begin the process of effective cultivation.

- **Get to know them well.** Find out what each board member does, professionally and otherwise. What are their passions? What other things do they commit personal time to? Learn what you can about their personal lives and families. The more that you get to know them personally, the more you can connect with them about their deepest and most sacred feelings and beliefs.

- **Start bonding.** Where appropriate, invite board members to your home or a location of common interest to interact socially. Let them see another side of you and vice versa. Also consider team-building activities that will force you and them to work together towards various outcomes.

- **Learn their biases.** Ask them about their general feelings about the organization. Is it something that they are proud to be associated with? What do they believe are its greatest strengths and biggest opportunities? Discuss their past experiences with your predecessor(s) and with other board members. Ask them about their top issues with the current company performance and culture.

These experiences will build equity and help your board see you as more than a distant employee that they have hired to direct their company. Should any blowback reach them from constituents, they will much likelier to cover your back and give you the benefit of the doubt than if you let things run their natural courses.

Your board can be a huge strategic asset. Not only do you want to win them over to your way of thinking and make them confident in your work, but you also want to be able to tap into their collective wisdom for insights and guidance.

In addition to these strategies, leaders would be wise to make sure that board members genuinely respect them. The following suggestions will help you engender the board's esteem and trust.

- **Lead your board.** Just as boards hold the CEO accountable to a set of standards and behaviors, the CEO must require the same of their board. Leaders must clearly communicate what they need from board members and then demand they do more than just show up for the meetings.

- **Lay out your plan.** Develop an initial plan that includes action steps and tangible deliverables. Get feedback on the plan and revise as needed. Then, monitor your progress against the plan and report using that as your basis. If you meet or exceed expectations, wonderful. If not, be willing to notate that and explain why you think that things have not progressed the way that you thought they would. Offer the board a modified plan as warranted. The more that you hold yourself accountable, the more respect and latitude you will garner.

- **Communicate early and often.** Develop and maintain a regular, planned communication schedule with your board. Update them on developments and don't hide concerns. Be forthright, clear, and responsive. Overcommunicate at first, so the board knows you get it and are on top of things. Then, with input and approval from the board chair, begin the process of weaning back a bit on the frequency and comprehensiveness of your updates.

Make sure to get a draft of the board agenda out to the key players well in advance of the meeting. Use these proactive encounters to flesh out, and seek alignment on, key issues and positions.

Also, board meetings don't have to only happen in the presence of the full board. A golden rule of board management is that the primary meeting takes place before the formal board meeting. Conduct individual phone calls or meetings with board members in advance of the actual board meeting to seek their input and advice.

- **Be prepared.** Never go into board meetings without knowing where your board stands on key issues. If there is bad news to share, air it out in smaller conversation rather than dropping a bomb in the middle of the conference table. This keeps the temperature lower and also keeps meeting minutes clear of perhaps the harshest comments and reactions. Remember: An unprepared leader is one who will not endure the test of time.

- **Make your meetings engaging.** Why can't board members look forward to their meetings? Aim to make meetings meaningful, productive and (where possible) enjoyable. Good attitudes bring out the best in people, which makes for easier conversation and decision making. To that end, makes sure to supply food and use a comfortable setting. Also use your time to grapple with real issues and leave the pettier details for e-mail and memos.

Finally, do what you can to fashion a board that can help you grow as a leader and advance the mission. Some leaders find themselves in the enviable position of being able to drive the selection process for their board. If that is your situation, make sure to choose wisely. Aim for diversity in such areas as thought, industry knowledge, skill, and experience. You would rather have people who will challenge your thinking and force you to make good decisions than folks who will mindlessly rubber-stamp your recommendations and add little value. If you find that you have strong opposition that cannot be managed or improved, do everything possible to have such members removed before they do the same to you.

CHAPTER 18

Become a Great Listener

If we were supposed to talk more than we listen,
we would have two tongues and one ear.

MARK TWAIN

I remember once attending a talk on communication. The speaker, whom we'll call Mr. S., is a life coach and communication expert. Mr. S. recalled his early years when he was a program coordinator for a large educational organization that required that he often meet with principals to sell his programs.

Mr. S. met with two men in short succession. One gentleman was gracious and well-meaning. He had a lengthy appointment but allowed himself to be interrupted by phone calls and other matters. Though they spent an hour together, the meeting felt short and unproductive. In the next school, Mr. S. had to wait for a while and was given but a few minutes with the principal. The man apologized for his lateness and brevity but made sure that during their time together, Mr. S's agenda was fully heard and responded to. It goes without saying that Mr. S. felt significantly more validated by the second man, despite the wait and their short time together.

To succeed in today's business world, leaders must be proactive, skilled listeners. Leaders who make themselves accessible for conversation and listen regularly are well informed of the goings-on in their workplaces. They better understand others' opinions and attitudes and can take this information into consideration when making decisions. By listening carefully, they also keep others' concerns in front of them and reduce the amount of negative conversation that makes its way to the water cooler or underground.

What can leaders do to become better listeners and gain the feedback, confidence, support and buy-in that they seek?

- **See eye-to-eye.** Eye contact is an important element of all face-to-face communication, even if you know the speaker well. By fixing your eyes on the speaker, you will avoid becoming distracted while also demanding genuine attention. Visibly put away possible distractors such as your phone. This communicates that there is nothing more important to you right now than this conversation.

- **Use receptive body language.** Without saying a word, our bodies communicate much about attitudes and feelings. We need to be aware of this in any conversation that we have. If seated, lean slightly forward to communicate attention. Nod or use other gestures or words that will encourage the speaker to continue.

- **Position yourself wisely.** Always be careful to maintain an appropriate distance between you and the speaker. Being too close may communicate pushiness or lack of respect. If you remain distant, however, you may be seen as cold or disinterested. Body postures matter too in most cultures. The crossing of one's arms or legs, for example, often conveys close-mindedness.

Leaders must be proactive, skilled listeners. Leaders who make themselves accessible for conversation and listen regularly are well informed of the goings-on in their workplaces.

- **Stop talking and start listening.** This is a most basic listening principle, and often the hardest to abide by. When somebody else is talking, it can be very tempting to jump in with a question or comment. This is particularly true when we seek to sound informed, insightful, or if we start to feel defensive due to the speaker's criticisms. Be mindful that a pause, even a long one, does not necessarily mean that the speaker has finished. Let the speaker continue in his or her own time; sometimes it takes a few moments to formulate what to say and how to say it. Never interrupt or finish a sentence for someone. Patient listening demonstrates that you respect others, which is the first step in building trust and rapport. Remember, if you desire to be listened to, give others the courtesy of listening to them first.

- **Humbly take on their point of view.** Approach each conversation from the vantage point of the speaker. Seek to empathize and to objectively consider their position, regardless of their rank. Be humble enough to listen carefully, even if you disagree with what is being said. Remember, those who confront and challenge you are ultimately the ones who help you stretch and develop most. True wisdom doesn't see opposition, only opportunity.

- **Summarize and clarify.** When the other person has finished talking, take a moment to restate and clarify what you have heard. Use language like, "So, to summarize, I think you said…" End by asking whether you heard correctly, which will encourage immediate feedback. Not only will this ensure the clearest takeaway on your end, but also help the speaker feel genuinely heard and valued. A strategically placed pause at some point in the feedback can be used to signal that you are carefully considering the message that was just shared.

- **Leave the door open.** Keep open the possibility of additional communication after this conversation has ended. You never know when new insights or concerns may emerge.

- **Thank them for approaching you.** Do not take any conversation for granted. For many employees, requesting a meeting requires that they summon much courage and rehearse their message time and again. Moreover, you probably learned something useful and meaningful during your talk: information or ideas that may help you as the leader. Few things go as far in building good will as a genuine expression of appreciation.

While all of the above strategies can help leaders make the most of listening opportunities, leaders also need to take steps to create a broader culture in which listening (and therefore communicating) is valued and desired. Cultures typically do not evolve on their own. They are the product of conscious decisions and modeled behaviors that, over time, become part of the fabric of communal and organizational life. Leaders who actively encourage others to speak and share their thoughts will be more likely to really know what people are thinking (including when they are upset), learn from the group's collective wisdom, strengthen morale, and increase worker motivation while also being able to learn.

SECTION 4

LEADING BY RELATING

CHAPTER 19

Build Strong, Balanced Relationships

*Much of leadership is about finding balance between
two often-conflicting activities: asserting authority and
responding to others' needs.*

BELLE LINDA HALPERN AND KATHY LUBAR

~

One summer after a couple of years on the job, I went out and bought a set of note cards. My goal was to surprise each teacher on the first day of faculty meetings with a special handwritten note. The text was largely the same for each note, with one unique line for every staff member that highlighted a personal quality. It read: "I really appreciate the way that you…" and would focus on something like a teacher's passion, creativity, contribution to the team, etc. I left each teacher a card in his or her box on the first day of faculty preservice meetings.

This was not the first thing that I left for the teachers. Often, I would leave treats or other "thinking of you" goodies as a way of demonstrating appreciation and goodwill. But I never got the same degree of positive feedback as I did that time with the notes. Many teachers commented on how much their note meant to them. Some posted it on the wall above their desks and looked at them often for inspiration.

The process of connecting with your professional team begins with becoming acquainted with them as individuals. Try to learn and understand their strengths and their goals, professional as well as personal. What are they really good at? What are they passionate about, both in and out of work? What do they want to achieve? People appreciate when you take an honest interest in them and demonstrate care. They also love it when you can identify specific qualities and behaviors that make them special in your eyes.

One way to learn more about your people is to schedule one-to-one meetings in your office. There should be no formal agenda, just a desire to get to know them better. You can also drop in at their workspace for an impromptu chat, or even meet up to go offsite together. I personally prefer the latter two options because they even out the playing field and help your coworker feel more relaxed and in control.

If you talk in their office or cubicle, use that opportunity to notice something special there, such as pictures that your coworker has displayed, an inspirational quote, or some cute collectibles on her desk. These could serve as interesting conversation builders and also give you valuable insights to tuck away for a later time. Meeting offsite offers a change of pace as well as more focused conversation, far removed from the office hubbub. Regardless of venue, seek to make connecting a regular part of your job routine. Let people know that you're committed to your relationship and seek to deepen it over time.

Once you have succeeded in developing positive relationships, it is more likely that people within the organization will candidly update you on internal developments, warn you about potential challenges or land mines, and even tolerate your mistakes more willingly. This can be very valuable, particularly at the beginning of your tenure.

There are other benefits to a strong boss-employee relationship. One is employees' job satisfaction, which can be up to two-and-a-half times higher when relations between the parties are strong.[28] Positive ties with the boss also positively correlated with employee motivation, morale, and loyalty. These help reduce workplace turnover, which can cost companies much in terms of replacement and training.

∿

If you have been promoted from a nonleadership position within your own company, a lot of things about your job are going to change, including your relationship with your coworkers. You are no longer peers. Of course, this

---

[28] Based on a 2004 Gallup poll: Gallup, Inc. "U.S. Workers Remain Largely Satisfied With Their Jobs." Gallup.com. November 27, 2007. Accessed February 22, 2017. http://www.gallup.com/poll/102898/us-workers-remain-largely-satisfied-their-jobs.aspx._

doesn't mean that you can't still be friendly with one another. It becomes all the more important, however, that future relationship building takes place without you compromising your standing as the boss. If you cross that line, you may very well run into one or more of the following problems:

> *Once you have succeeded in developing positive relationships, it is more likely that people within the organization will candidly update you on internal developments, warn you about potential challenges or landmines, and even tolerate your mistakes more willingly.*

- **Feeling dissed.** A boss needs to know that his decision is final and will be respected. Bosses who make friends with employees simply cannot expect to be treated with the same level of deference and cooperation as those who maintain healthy boundaries.

- **Tainted decision-making.** Leaders must be able to make important decisions that are consistent with the company's values, protocols, and procedures. Their judgment can't be clouded by close relationships that may sway them to bend the rules. Those who manage to maintain their objectivity may still be judged as playing favorites.

- **Compromised privacy.** The hallmark of a close friendship is the sharing of private information. We lower our guard and tell our friends things that are not meant for public consumption. When such friendships form between boss and worker, it can be difficult to refrain from unloading work-related issues or confiding about other employees' shortcomings.

The key point here is to learn to be professionally friendly. Let people know how much you appreciate their work and get to know them as people. But stop short of becoming so friendly as to blur the lines and complicate the relationship.

~

Despite your best efforts to build relationships, it is possible and even likely that some staffers will still have a hard time getting used to you and your style (it happens to the best of us, don't take it personally!) or simply not want to conform to the changes being asked of them. These people may choose to demonstrate their displeasure through water cooler chatter or worse.

Without a doubt, it would be a mistake to allow this to continue in the spirit of being the nice guy and hoping that they'll come around. These behaviors and attitudes need to be addressed early on and in a clear and firm manner. By identifying and dealing with bad apples, you may be able to anticipate and diffuse a lot of problems that they might cause before things become worse. Your proactive approach will send a clear message that certain behaviors will not be tolerated. It will also be appreciated by the rest of your staff who may be even more fed up with such negativity than you are.

CHAPTER 20

Hear It and Get on with It

We all need people who will give us feedback.
That's how we improve.

BILL GATES

~

As a leader, especially one who promotes open communication, you will certainly be the recipient of some unflattering feedback. The comments may focus in on your leadership style, specific actions or comments of yours, your attitudes, or some combination thereof. Even if the remark was delivered with constructive intent, you might resent the message. Perhaps you will seek opportunities to get back at the source of your reproach, or at least gain satisfaction from his or her next slip up.

All of this is normal. Some may call it natural or even healthy. But as someone who has received his fair share of criticism over the years, my suggestion is that you get what you can from the comments and then move on, as quickly and completely as possible.

There is nothing to be gained from harboring negative thoughts. Nor does it pay to hold out for some form of vindication. The best form of payback that you can deliver is doing a better job the next time and gaining that person's admiration.

But it's not about getting payback anyway. Such thinking is limiting and focuses you completely in the wrong direction. When we think of retribution or even simply hold onto some form of animosity, we allow ourselves to remain stuck and focus on events that have already occurred. The best way forward is to be future-thinking and to see how you can make today and every day the very best and productive yet in your career.

I am not suggesting that all criticism is fair and well-intentioned. Sometimes it is motivated by insecurity. At other times, it may be driven by jealousy or even anger. Certainly, you are not obligated to gladly and willingly accept everyone's slap on the cheek and then turn your head for one more on the other side. But we must be able to separate the intent and words of the criticizer from what we ultimately do with her message.

Keep in mind that almost every form of criticism—even that which is born from bad intent—can teach us something powerful about ourselves. Certainly, if someone has it out for you, he will seize upon an area of perceived or accepted weakness to build a credible case. When an

> *The best form of payback that you can deliver is doing a better job the next time and gaining that person's admiration.*

attribute or behavior is singled out, let me assure you that there's at least some kernel of truth in what's being said. Doing something about that issue, including finding out what's rubbing people the wrong way and taking steps to improve in that area, will serve you admirably long into the future— probably well after your relationship with the other party has ended.

The next time that someone approaches you with some unwanted feedback, consider doing the following:

- **Listen well.** As discussed above, the single most important part of any relationship or exchange is to be a good listener. Hear the person out without interruption. Then mirror back what you heard for clarification. If there is something that you disagree with, hold it until the end. This way you validate the message sender and open further lines of communication.

- **Respond carefully.** Try to avoid sounding defensive. Leave your ego to the side and accept warranted concerns as well as viable advice. If you are unsure about the validity of feedback or what to do with it, ask for time to respond. Make sure to get back to the other party in a timely fashion and with a real game plan (see below). Ask for feedback about the plan.

- **Thank the person.** Let him or her know that you appreciate the fact that he or she brought this matter to you and didn't go around you. It would have been easier, less risky, and more comfortable to do so. Let the person know that you appreciate this growth opportunity given to you.

- **Seek more feedback.** Chances are that others also have opinions about the matter at hand. Find others whose opinion you trust and try to gauge the broader truth. Just how widespread is this concern?

- **Do something.** This may be the hardest part. No one likes to change, especially if we already have a plan in place and are well along in its execution. Character change is even harder. Seek to identify, alone or with a trusted confidant or coach, a set of actions that can help you grow as a leader. Then make sure to get back with the concerned party about what you have decided so that he or she feels validated and also does not add more grist to the mill.

We all want to hear that we're doing well. Feedback is the breakfast of champions, and positive comments can direct more wind behind our sails. But no one wants to be an emperor without clothes, or, worse yet, a dethroned emperor. Whether the unflattering feedback that you receive was solicited or not, be sure to make good use of it so that you can lead an inspired and engaged team forward.

CHAPTER 21

Be Open and Honest

To be persuasive, we must be believable; to be believable, we must be credible; to be credible, we must be truthful.

EDWARD R. MURROW

~

One of the hardest talks that I have had to deliver took place right before the beginning of my third year as head of school. It was at the back-to-school full faculty meeting, and I needed to clear the air about an issue that was on many people's minds.

The issue was me. Not that I necessarily had done anything so terrible that required addressing. But I knew that our insular, largely veteran faculty was still struggling with the transition from their previous boss and the new style of leadership that I represented. My message was simple and direct. I validated the feelings of those who continued to pine for a bygone era and let them know that I was prepared to do whatever I could to ensure the smoothest pathway forward.

After the talk, a veteran teacher approached me. He thanked me for my words and told me that I had said what needed to be said to acknowledge and validate. It was now time to move on to what we needed to achieve. And we achieved quite a bit that year; perhaps more than in my previous two years combined.

The ability to take an honest look at a situation and take the necessary steps to rectify it—even if it means admitting error and/or acknowledging weakness—is crucial for every leader's effectiveness. Frequently, however, we see just the opposite occur. In many instances, our first response is to deny problems or mistakes or conjure up excuses to justify their occurrence. Nobody wants to appear as foolish or ill-informed. This is particularly true of leaders, who tend to feel that they must always act justifiably or lose credibility.

Fans of the 1970s sitcom *Happy Days* fondly remember the heroics and antics of Arthur "Fonzie" Fonzarelli. Fonzie was the quintessential cool guy and always seemed to show up at the right time to save Richie and friends from trouble. But even the great Fonzie made mistakes, and when he did, he demonstrated a deep inability to admit his errors. The first two words, "I was," came out without issue. When he reached the word, "wrong," his face became contorted and pained. Try as he might (and he did try), the Fonz simply could not proclaim error. "I was wrrr-rrr-rrr..." was as far as it went. Through comic relief, Fonzie exemplified a human weakness that is often expressed most deeply by those in positions of leadership and perceived strength.

The ability to take an honest look at a situation and take the necessary steps to rectify it—even if it means admitting error and/or acknowledging weakness—is crucial for every leader's effectiveness.

Error is as central to the human condition as any other quality. We all make mistakes and will do so every day of our lives. We must be able to accept our errors for what they are and have the self-confidence and integrity to admit them. Our ability and willingness to do this, perhaps more than anything else, will allow us to build and maintain the trust of those we lead.

Business leaders routinely make decisions based on imperfect information and judgment. They may get blindsided by a competitor's response or underestimate the challenges in developing and selling products. They may misread constituent readiness for change or the impact of a new program or system. By wholeheartedly acknowledging our errors and misjudgments, rather than avoiding responsibility or offering up excuses, leaders can limit damage and get back on the right course. Remember, you don't drown by falling in water. You drown by staying there.

What prevents leaders from apologizing freely, from owning up to their mistakes and taking full responsibility for them? One contributor, no doubt, is the cultural axiom that leaders, particularly aspiring ones, should hide weaknesses and errors.[29] Many leaders think that they need to be near-perfect to garner others' respect.

In truth, it is healthy for leaders to admit their wrongdoings; such practice can actually increase their legitimacy among their coworkers. To admit error is to demonstrate courage, and people want courageous leaders—people who will make the tough calls and to take responsibility for them. Courage also begets courage; followers are more likely to make their own tough decisions and to take responsibility for them when their supervisors model that same behavior. Have their backs, and they will more likely have yours.

Of course, no one should be acknowledging error too often. That would mean that there are fundamental problems with your information-gathering or decision-making skills. But assuming that you do not exceed the normative error quotient typically allowed to leaders, particularly new ones, you should be fine so long as you own up to your errors.

In terms of the actual apology, follow these simple rules to maximize its effect.

- **Apologize sincerely.** Saying, "I am sorry" must communicate genuine regret for your behavior and a heartfelt wish that you had acted differently.

- **Avoid excuses.** State your error directly, without justification. To the listener's ear, excuses feel like an attempt to validate the wrongdoing.

- **Take complete ownership.** Don't shift the blame ("I apologize that *you misunderstood me*," "I am sorry that *you felt that way*," etc.). Stating (or even implying) that the other person was partly responsible for what occurred will lead them to consider you disingenuous and perhaps even accusatory. And that is no way to apologize.

- **State how you intend to fix things.** Articulating your intent to correct matters, including an action plan of intended steps, will do

---

[29] See Guthrie, Doug. "Creative Leadership: Humility and Being Wrong." *Forbes*. June 06, 2012. Accessed February 22, 2017. http://www.forbes.com/sites/dougguthrie/2012/06/01/creative-leadership-humility-and-being-wrong/.

wonders to convince the listener of your sincerity. Your plan should be simple and realistic.

- **Follow through.** Few things damage morale more than when a leader sets expectations for personal change and then does not follow through. In many ways, it is worse than not having apologized in the first place. When leaders do not act as promised, employees question not only their courage and will, but also their trustworthiness.

CHAPTER 22

Get out There

Coming together is a beginning. Keeping together is progress.
Working together is success.

HENRY FORD

~

Another way for leaders to develop a strong bond with their people right out of the gate is to roll up their sleeves and get to work. Not just on their own work, but the work of their direct reports, as well as their reports' reports. Take time to sit in various offices and seats within the organization and seek to develop new skills and make connections on different levels. Ask about existing challenges within the company and develop empathy for those who are tasked with addressing them regularly. Brainstorm with staff about how best to address these issues to optimize performance. By bringing yourself down to your people, you will gain their admiration as someone who really seeks to know their situations and improve them.

Of course, another significant benefit is the knowledge that you will learn about parts of the company about which you are presently unfamiliar. Your newfound perspective will add insight to decision-making processes large and small.

Another, more sustainable approach to bonding with employees is to connect with them actively on a regular basis. Hewlett Packard (HP) founders William Hewlett and David Packard used a strategy that has become known as MBWA, or *Management by Wandering Around*. As its name implies, MBWA requires regular walking throughout the workplace. It offers many benefits to leaders and their employees, such as:

- **Awareness.** Walking around can give you a better understanding of the functions and processes around you. This could be crucial as you begin the decision-making process and want to be able to keep all important information under consideration.

- **Relationship building.** Your workers will start to feel that you care about what they do and who they are, and will come to appreciate you for it. It will also raise workplace morale, knowing that you are committed to them and their success.

- **Approachability.** The more that you are around, the more that people begin to view you as another person and not simply a distant boss. That, coupled with your proximity, makes it likelier that they'll tell you what's really going on. You may learn about issues before they become real problems.

- **New ideas.** Often, creative thoughts occur "in the moment" and not at formal meetings. Your presence promotes casual discussions, so people will more likely feel free to come to you with their ideas.

> *Leaders have to walk a fine line in the workplace. On the one hand, people want them to be interested and involved. On the other hand, they can easily wear out their welcome by becoming meddlesome and stealing the process from those who were tasked to complete it.*

To achieve this, you must use the walk-through strategically. Here are some other tips can help you get the most from your strolls:

- **Stroll calmly.** You want to get around but should not convey hurriedness. Staffers should feel that you're happy to be there and that this was your intended destination. Project a sense of relaxed calmness as you interact and you will get people to open up and respond naturally.

- **Ask for feedback and be a good listener.** Let everyone know that you want to hear what they have to say to improve the workplace and strenghten performance. Hold back as much as possible from saying what you think, at least for now.

- **Be judicious in your observations.** If you notice something positive, offer a compliment. If you see something that concerns you, bite your tongue and talk to the person later, in private.

- **Use your time wisely.** Don't spend a disproportionate amount of time in one particular area. Make sure to talk to different people at different levels within the organization. Everyone should feel you are approachable and genuinely interested in them.

Though a leader's direct involvement can genuinely energize her team or company, she should be careful not to become *too* involved. This will cheapen the effect and make people feel as if you are watching them closely.

I made that mistake once at the beginning of my principal tenure. I would regularly come out to join staffers who managed the carpool line, thinking that such involvement would help the teachers and offer me another opportunity to engage with parents and students. All of that was fine until I started taking over the process and stepping on some toes as I did. I got the hint when my associate principal told me that it was "beneath me" to be out there barking carpool instructions. That was her nice way of saying that I had gone a bit too far and had worn out my welcome.

Leaders have to walk a fine line in the workplace. On the one hand, people want them to be interested and involved. On the other hand, they can easily wear out their welcome by becoming meddlesome and stealing the process from those who were tasked to complete it. So long as leaders take the necessary measures to remain in others' good graces, they will find that their time in the trenches will be time very well spent.

CHAPTER 23

Take on Others' Perspectives

*The more we can get together and talk about various
perspectives, feelings, beliefs, the better.*

WILLIAM P. LEAHY

~

In his book, *The Seven Habits of Highly Effective People*,[30] Steven Covey included an ambiguous optical illusion that is open to different interpretations.[31] To some readers, the image is that of an old lady looking downward, wearing a shawl and a fur coat. To others, it is the portrait of a young, aristocratic woman with her head turned sideways. Covey uses the image to speak about paradigms and the way that our past thinking and inclinations can significantly alter how we look at things and respond to situations.

I was reminded of this recently during a conversation with an old colleague from a school where I used to teach. Not only was she one of the school's teachers, but she was also the activities director. She recalled that one winter weekend, the school had gone on a retreat, and faculty was able to attend with their families. I came along with my wife and three young children. As my colleague remembered it, the kids were having a blast during a ski outing and had managed to get themselves all full of snow, much to the chagrin of their father. My colleague had been pleased that the children were so wet; to her, it meant that they were enjoying themselves. I, on the other hand, chose to focus on the involved cleanup and clothes changing that awaited me.

As we know, different viewpoints are based on the unique approaches, biases, and inclinations that we bring to situations. Where we get ourselves into trouble, however, particularly in the workplace, is when we assume

---

[30] Covey, Stephen R. *The Seven Habits of Highly Effective People: Restoring the Character Ethic*. New York: Simon and Schuster, 1989.

[31] "Paradigms." *Leaders Are Readers*. July 20, 2010. Accessed February 22, 2017. https://goeagle.wordpress.com/tag/paradigm/.

that our perspective is the only one that exists, let alone the only one that matters.

Such narrow thinking can be even more damaging for leaders. Not only does it prevent them from grasping opportunities and identifying challenges that only others are attuned to, but it can also lead to discontent and frustration in others who do not feel heard or valued.

How can we make sure to avoid such thinking and ensure that we not only become more mindful of other views but actively seek them out?

First, we should understand where our resistance to such thinking comes from. Why are we so programmed to block out the possibility of other thoughts and perspectives and to defend our own stances with such vigor?

One factor is our inherent desire to be right. Being right affirms and inflates our self-worth. It's part of being human to want to have our way, to be correct and use that to control others. By necessity, we come to believe that anyone who disagrees with us must be wrong, because we assume that only one of us could be correct, and it definitely isn't the other person.

Some argue (correctly, in my opinion,) that this craving is reinforced by our educational system. Historically, the focus in school has been about independent work and our ability as individuals to demonstrate mastery and correctness. (This has changed somewhat with a twenty-first-century education focus on collaboration and idea sharing, but we are far from a genuine paradigm shift in this regard.) Our schools reward correct answers with higher grades, which can impact subsequent schooling and employment opportunities.

Another culprit is the talking heads of political debate. We regularly view debates over issues on talk shows and in political forums where the end goal is not to arrive at a mutually beneficial solution, but rather to ram views down each other's throats in a zero-sum game and see who possesses better one-liners and debating tactics.

> *Even if we were to argue that only one perspective can stand in the end, why not create a culture in which dissent is valued as a means of fleshing out ideas and vetting options to help arrive at the very best solution?*

But if we are honest with ourselves, we know that being right is not an absolute position. Particularly in the work environment, there often can be more than one correct position about how to approach something. And even if we were to argue that only one perspective can stand in the end, why not create a culture in which dissent is valued as a means of fleshing out ideas and vetting options to help arrive at the very best solution?

So how can we, as leaders, become better listeners and more open to others' ideas? The following are some ideas to consider:

- **Keep your mind open.** One of the easiest ways to fall into the I-am-right trap is to determine the decision or direction before discussing things with others. Even if you then bring the issue to another person or the group, you will want to defend your position. Instead, remind yourself that there are likely multiple approaches and perspectives, and there's a good chance that someone else's views will help you clarify and solidify your own, or perhaps open you up to a whole new perspective.

- **Create opportunities for conversation.** Don't wait for issues or concerns to arise before bringing folks together to discuss them. Establish regular meeting times to reflect upon and solve issues. If there are none, present hypothetical dilemmas for everyone to review and debate. This offers the added benefit of allowing people to consider solutions without having to defend past actions or positions, removing personal bias.

- **Take on others' perspectives.** Think about issues from the perspective of those who are affected. The rank-and-file will often be more focused on or concerned with how decisions will affect them, their jobs, and job security, and leaders would be wise to keep those issues at the forefront of their minds. As they are speaking, be empathetic and seek to objectively consider their position. As Stephen Covey phrased it, "seek to understand before being understood."

- **Do a role reversal.** Clearly state your position, your point of view, while your "opponent" listens carefully for the details, taking notes if needed. Then your partner explains his or her position, while you listen. No discussion or interrupting allowed. Then switch roles and pretend to be the other person presenting *their* argument. Take note of what it feels to be in that position, and see if the other's point of view makes more sense, now that you are in his or her shoes.

- **Ask yourself, "Do I want to be right or do I want to be happy?"** At the end of the day, you often will have to choose between the satisfaction that comes with being correct and being happy. As you relinquish self-centeredness and look to the needs of those around you, you develop intimacy and connectedness. As the Canadian writer and leadership speaker Robin Sharma once said, "The business of business is relationships; the business of life is human connection."[32]

---

[32] "ReTHINK: Interview with Robin Sharma." GeniusTribes Training Resources. Accessed February 22, 2017. http://rethink-redefine.blogspot.com/2012/10/rethink-interview-with-robin-sharma.html.

SECTION 5

DEEPENING
THE BOND

CHAPTER 24

Make Your Feedback Personal

Everyone has an invisible sign hanging from their neck saying,
"Make me feel important." Never forget this message when
working with people.

MARY KAY ASH

~

It is not a secret that job satisfaction in this country is not where it should be. A 2014 Conference Board report says that the majority of Americans (52.3 percent) are unhappy at work.[33] What makes our workers happiest? The Conference Board says that "interest in work" provides satisfaction to 59 percent of the workplace. Even more fulfilling is "people at work," which 60.6 percent said they liked. Similarly, an expansive study by Boston Consulting Group found that the number one factor for employee happiness on the job is being appreciated for their work.[34] (There are many other factors that also contribute to workplace happiness, such as strong alignment between skills and task, passion for the job, as well as fair, if not robust, compensation.)

The question, then, is this. If interpersonal relationships and the expression of appreciation are so important to employees, why aren't leaders spending more time on these (as evidenced by the high rate of employment-related unhappiness)? It would appear that the following factors and mindsets are to blame:

- **It takes too much time.** Leaders are busy people with many responsibilities. Their days are filled with meetings to attend, tasks to

[33] "Job Satisfaction: 2014 Edition."The Conference Board. Accessed February 22, 2017. http://www.conference-board.org/publications/publicationdetail.cfm?publicationid=2785.

[34] Strack, Rainer, Carsten Von Der Linden, Mike Booker, and Andrea Strohmeyer. "Decoding Global Talent." www.bcgperspectives.com. October 06, 2014. Accessed February 22, 2017. https://www.bcgperspectives.com/content/articles/human_resources_leadership_decoding_global_talent/

complete, and employees to
oversee and evaluate. There
simply isn't the time (or so
they think) to share praise
and appreciation, particularly
to craft words that are sin-
cere and personal.

> *Appreciation has to
> be expressed, even if
> it means taking time
> from something else or
> delegating some current
> responsibilities*

- **I need to get to know my
  people.** It's hard to express such feelings to people you don't know
  all that well, particularly on a personal level. Getting to know people
  takes time, effort, and a genuine desire to connect with others. It's
  easier said than done.

- **If I praise one person, I need to do so for everyone else.**
  Often, we get stuck in the mindset of equality leadership, believing
  that if we demonstrate approval of one employee, we must do so for
  all. We fear that it may come across as preferential treatment to only
  acknowledge some of our colleagues. And, as we noted above, who
  has the time to praise them all?

- **I don't need it; why should they?** Leaders are typically hard-
  working folks who earned their posts in part because of deep levels
  of commitment and self-motivation. They think that their people
  should be similarly motivated and that praise and other external
  influences are to be avoided.

- **I don't want to create smugness and complacency.** Perhaps
  some leaders worry that excessive praise will lead to slacking and
  other adverse effects. People who think that they are succeeding
  often take their feet off of the gas pedal and fail to achieve to
  previous levels.

- **Is it such a big deal?** While research clearly demonstrates the
  connection between recognition and job satisfaction, it may not be
  clear that satisfaction at the workplace really matters. Who cares if
  they're happy, they may think, so long as the work gets done?

Without question, such thinking is both narrow and counterproductive.
Logic dictates that satisfied, appreciated employees make for happy,

productive workplaces. They are likelier to be engaged in their work, to convey positivity to others, and to remain focused and determined when things get tough because they know that their efforts are being noticed and appreciated. They will also likely stick around when other opportunities present themselves, cutting down on recruitment and training costs, not to mention the impact of losing a key player in the middle of an important project. To those leaders who think that they did not ever need some support and appreciation to get the job done, I ask how much more they could have achieved with more fuel to fire their engines.

The implications for leaders is that appreciation *has* to be expressed, even if it means taking time from something else or delegating some current responsibilities. Donald Peterson, former chairman of Ford Motor Company, said the most important ten minutes of his day were spent boosting the people around him. He understood that his people needed to be stroked and used a few minutes each day to get his employees charged up for success.

So, take the time to get to know everyone well. This way you can offer targeted, meaningful, personal feedback to everyone in your employ. If you do not oversee certain people, ask their supervisors about their performance and special qualities. And then find ways to express them. Orally is good; in writing is even better, because they can show it off and refer back to it during tough moments. Don't worry about them becoming smug or complacent. Continue to set goals with them and hold them accountable. That will keep the honest, focused, and growth-oriented.

Mark Twain famously said that he could go for two months on one strong compliment. If Twain, with all of his success, notoriety, and acclaim, was so dependent on others' opinions, think about how much your well-delivered and considerate comments can do for the people who you are paying to help you grow and advance your business.

CHAPTER 25

Don't Let E-mail Become E-fail

> I was discussing the use of e-mail and how impersonal it
> can be; how people will now e-mail someone across the
> room rather than go and talk to them.
>
> MARGARET J. WHEATLEY

~

If there was one area where I got hit hard at the beginning of my tenure as
a school leader, it was communication. The first complaint related to my
style, which was seen as being too impersonal. I was heavily involved with
my BlackBerry, texting and regularly e-mailing to reach out to or respond
to various constituents (even in meetings and while sitting in on classroom
observations). Though my objectives were lofty—I wanted to share ideas
and be as readily accessible and responsive as possible—some saw me as
being too digitized and distracted. This was, in part, because my predecessor
rarely e-mailed. Nor did he own a smartphone or text much.

We all know the reasons that we type so many of our correspondences
instead of writing them down on a piece of paper. It's often faster, it's neater,
and it can easily be saved and categorized for future reference without paper
sifting and clutter. Electronic communications can be shared far and wide
and allow us to reach out and reply when it works for us, not having to be
concerned as much with the other's schedule and readiness to communicate.

Despite the many benefits of e-communication, it can also present some
serious downsides. These include:

- **Misinterpretation.** A great deal of the way that we normally share
  information and ideas when face-to-face with another is through
  nonverbal communication. Inflections, hand gestures, facial tone,
  body positioning and the like say much about how each party is
  receiving and responding to each other, as well as their passion for

the information and ideas being shared. Without hearing a voice or seeing nonverbal cues (such as with e-mail), people struggle to properly discern the intended meaning, tone, value and emphasis.

A study by Professors Justin Kruger (New York University) and Nicholas Epley (University of Chicago) sought to determine how well sarcasm is detected in electronic messages.[35] The study found that not only do e-mail senders overestimate their ability to communicate feelings, but recipients also overrate their ability to decode those feelings correctly.

- **Impersonal touch.** No matter how thoughtfully an e-mail is crafted, its digital nature makes it feel distant and impersonal. You simply cannot compare the feel of an e-mail with that of a face-to-face chat or a phone call.

- **Raising the temperature.** For most of us, distance makes it feel safer to "yell" or to be critical. We can more easily muster up the gumption to criticize when we are typing words on our personal keyboards than when we have to look someone in the eye and share our feelings. Furthermore, the prospect of instantaneous communication creates an urgency that pressures e-mailers to think and write quickly, which can lead to carelessness.

- **You can't get it back.** The immediate nature of e-mail makes it easy to forget that our words matter and can come back to bite us. (I suggest that you never send any e-mail with potentially negative implications without first showing it to one or two trusted colleagues for feedback). Not only must we worry about how our message will be processed in the moment, but there is also a chance that it will be forwarded or printed for others to see as well.

> *We have to be able to build healthy relationships. This requires a healthy dose of ongoing, in-person interactions.*

---

[35] Kruger, Justin, Nicholas Epley, Jason Parker, Jason, and Zhi-Wen Ng. "Egocentrism over E-mail: Can We Communicate as Well as We Think?" *Journal of Personality and Social Psychology* 89, no. 6 (2005): 925-36.

- **Keeping your distance.** Perhaps worst of all, e-mail, instant messaging (IM) and other e-communiqués maintain the distance between colleagues, sometimes even when only a wall or cubicle separate them physically. It's often easier to fire off a response than to get up and share a few words. You may not want to disturb your busy coworkers, especially if they are in another conversation or on the phone, and that is laudable. Still, it's important to not fall into the habit of remaining distant. Personal rapport keeps relationships strong, even in the face of conflict.

As our jobs involve working with and getting things done with people, we have to be able to build healthy relationships. This requires a healthy dose of ongoing, in-person interactions to get to know each other in real terms and understand how we each tick.

CHAPTER 26

Develop Your Emotional Intelligence

When dealing with people, remember you are not dealing with creatures of logic, but creatures of emotion.

DALE CARNEGIE

~

Chip Kelly caught the NFL by storm when he took over as Philadelphia Eagles head coach before the 2013 season following a successful run in college. Less than three years later, a perceived lack of emotional intelligence (EQ) on Kelly's part was largely to blame for his firing with one game left on the Eagles' regular season schedule.

During the press conference, Eagles CEO Jeffrey Lurie spoke about his vision for the team's next leader. "You've got to open your heart to players and everybody you want to achieve peak performance," Lurie said. "I would call it a style of leadership that values information and all of the resources that are provided and at the same time values emotional intelligence. I think in today's world, a combination of all those factors creates the best chance to succeed."

~

Often, the biggest obstacle for a new leader has little to do with how well she knows the job or whether she possesses the right technical skills. In fact, most leadership experts identify poor interpersonal qualities and practices as the main reason many new leaders stumble out of the gate. They suggest that such relational transgressions as not communicating often, not being available for people on a consistent basis, and being unpredictable emotionally are primary contributors to new leaders failing to gain traction.

These and other negative interpersonal behaviors may mean that a person is weak in the area of Emotional Intelligence (EQ). EQ refers to a person's ability to understand and manage his or her personal emotions and interpersonal conduct, as well as those of the people around him or her. People who rank high in EQ are in tune with their feelings and emotions and can accurately predict how they might affect other people.

EQ is an important quality for leaders in particular to possess. Leaders need to have a good sense of what others are thinking and feeling while also staying in firm control of their situational responses. This is particularly true in times of challenge. People prefer leaders who control themselves and calmly assess situations over those who lose control when under stress. Explosive behavior also stifles open communication and causes staff to walk on eggshells.

EQ has become popularized through the research and writings of psychologist Daniel Goleman.[36] Goleman lists five primary elements of emotional intelligence:

1. Self-awareness

2. Self-regulation

3. Internal motivation

4. Empathy

5. Social skills

Leaders who are *self-aware* are in check with their emotions. They understand what they are feeling and can identify the triggers behind their emotions. They also have a good sense of how different emotions and reactions impact those around them.

Self-aware leaders can list their strengths and weaknesses. They know what they do well, as well as where they struggle and need help. Such awareness tends to humble them, as they recognize that they simply are not great at everything. This, in turn, lends to a more collaborative work environment.

To improve your self-awareness, consider taking the time to identify your emotional triggers. How did a certain comment or response make you feel? What emotion was activated in a particular situation? Why was that so? In

---

[36] Goleman, Daniel. *Emotional Intelligence*. New York: Bantam Books, 1995.

general, how well equipped are you to react to different scenarios? The more aware that you are about yourself when you are not in the moment, the better you will be able to respond when you actually need to.

Self-regulation (being in control of one's emotions and reactions) helps us avoid the kinds of serious, hurtful comments or negative actions that can set us back and damage relationships.

> *Leaders need to have a good sense of what others are thinking and feeling while also staying in firm control of their situational responses. This is particularly true in times of challenge.*

Leaders who self-regulate effectively tend to be more flexible and committed to personal accountability. Research shows that most people don't want to work for hostile bosses, regardless of the pay.

Leaders can improve their ability to self-regulate by looking first in the mirror. Before blaming others for errors, take the time to see what you may have done to contribute to a problem, either directly or indirectly. Taking responsibility will help you react more evenly and fairly.

As noted above, consider practicing being in challenging situations before they occur. Run various scenarios through your mind and determine the best course of action in each case. While you cannot predict every possible situation, advance practice and consideration will help you remain calmer, more composed, and on target when things begin to escalate.

Lastly, take the time to review your values often, to the point where you can recite them by heart and offer examples of how they play out in the workplace and elsewhere. The more that you are in touch with your values, the likelier you will feel synergy and inner calm, even when times get tough.

The next element of EQ is *internal motivation*. Leaders who are internally motivated work consistently toward their goals and hold extremely high standards for the quality of their work. Their motivation comes from a variety of sources, including an inner drive to succeed and a quest for the material and other benefits that success will bring.

Sometimes our motivation can wane when we fail to see results or encounter resistance. Leaders can counter this effect by finding at least one good thing about every situation. It might be something small, like a new contact, or something with long-term benefits, such as a meaningful lesson learned.

Empathy refers to a person's ability to put himself in someone else's situation. They can relate deeply with those around them and offer guidance, support, and comfort when things go awry. In the words of Daniel Pink, "Empathy is about standing in someone else's shoes, feeling with his or her heart, seeing with his or her eyes. Not only is empathy hard to outsource and automate, but it makes the world a better place." Empathetic leaders help develop the people on their team, give balanced, constructive feedback, and offer a listening ear to those who need it.

The result of empathy is positive energy and synergy. Stephen Covey said it this way: "When you show deep empathy toward others, their defensive energy goes down, and positive energy replaces it. That's when you can get more creative in solving problems."[37] If you want to earn the respect and loyalty of your team, be empathic and show that you care. We noted above how research also shows that caring bosses drive increased productivity and promote employee retention.

Leaders can become more empathetic by seeking to put themselves in others' positions and looking at things from their vantage point. Try to step into an impartial role in which you do not try to justify or criticize, but rather to understand.

The last element of EQ is *social skills.* To be effective, leaders must have a solid understanding of how their emotions and actions affect the people around them. The better a leader relates to and works with others, the more successful he or she will be.

Empathy, together with social skills, comprise *social intelligence*, which is the interpersonal part of emotional intelligence. Socially intelligent leaders do more than just make people happier at work. According to Goleman, a survey of employees at seven hundred companies revealed that the majority said that a supportive boss mattered more to them than how much money they earned.[38]

Leaders who have good social skills communicate well, and not only when

---

[37] Covey, Stephen R. *The Seven Habits of Highly Effective People: Restoring the Character Ethic.* New York: Simon and Schuster, 1989.

things are looking up. They find positives in people's work and make regular deposits through praise and recognition. They are also good at managing change and resolving conflicts diplomatically. Conflict resolution involves acknowledging the conflict (rather than ignoring or suppressing it), discussing its impact, and then agreeing to a peaceful resolution that puts the team first.

Socially intelligent leadership begins with engagement; disengaged leaders simply can't put others at ease. An engaged leader, on the other hand, can discern how people feel and why they feel that way. He or she can then express appropriate concern and encourage more positive thinking.

---

[38] Goleman, Daniel. *Social Intelligence: The New Science of Human Relationships*. New York: Bantam Books, 2006.

CHAPTER 27

The Importance of Building Trust

The glue that holds all relationships together—including the relationship between the leader and the led—is trust, and trust is based on integrity.

BRIAN TRACY

~

Perhaps the most trusted American of all time was George Washington. Washington led our nation militarily and then politically during its troubled infancy, maintaining his vision and composure throughout a painful period of deprivation and uncertainty. Even after winning the American War of Independence, his country was deeply divided. About one third of the nation supported the new regime. Another third was neutral. The final third remained loyal to the King of England.

Washington led this divided country with resolve and integrity. Though aloof to a fault, he retained the people's trust because he acted with humility and not self-righteousness. Personal gain was not his goal. Instead, the general-turned-president focused his energies on maintaining and strengthening the principles of a democratic republic. This is why he was dubbed "The American Cincinnatus." Like the famous Roman, he won a war and became a private citizen instead of seeking power or riches as a reward. He insisted on simple titles, such as "Mr. President," rather than anything that spoke of aristocracy and grandeur.

~

Leaders in all contexts must build trust to achieve their goals. In fact, some, like business consultant Cynthia Olmstead, maintain that the fundamental difference between the enterprises and change initiatives that succeed and those that fail depends largely on whether there is a meaningful degree of trust within the organization.[39] People in high-trust relationships communicate well, don't second-guess one another, understand why they are doing things, and are willing to go the extra mile to ensure that goals are met. In the words of Stephen R. Covey, "When the trust account is high, communication is easy, instant, and effective."[40]

But what exactly is trust? For many of us, it's one of those "feel" terms that are hard to define. Of course, if we lack a common definition of the term, we can't effectively discuss it, let alone seek to create it in our workplaces.

In essence, trust is a feeling of security that you have, based on the belief that someone or something is knowledgeable, reliable, good, honest, and effective. At the least, the person or thing possess(es) a meaningful combination of some of these attributes. When applied to human relationships, trust develops when people interact and like the results, in terms of the quality of what they get (information, service, companionship, etc.) and the way in which it is presented and/or delivered.

Think, for example, about someone who advises you, such as your financial planner. He or she may get your business initially because of a strong reference or a solid interview. But the planner will begin to earn your trust if you are consistently satisfied with the quality of their advice and decisions, and you feel that he or she is acting in your best interests.

Let's explore this a bit further. In her book, which she co-authored with Ken Blanchard and Martha Lawrence, Olmstead speaks of four core aspects of trust, which she labeled *ABCD*, or Able, Believable, Connected, and Dependable.[41]

1. **Able** refers to your capacity for the task. Do you know your stuff and get results? Can and do you use your skills to support others' work? And do you demonstrate a growth mindset to learn things that you presently don't know so well?

2. **Believable** people know how to keep confidences. They don't talk behind people's backs, and they act with sincerity and

---

[39] Blanchard, Ken, and Blanchard, Scott. "Do Your Employees Trust You?" Fast Company. April 26, 2013. Accessed February 22, 2017. http://www.fastcompany.com/3008858/do-your-employees-trust-you.

[40] Covey, Stephen R. *The Seven Habits of Highly Effective People: Restoring the Character Ethic*. New York: Simon and Schuster, 1989: 188.

integrity. When they err, they willingly admit it. They also do not hide their lack of knowledge.

3. **Connected** people work well with others. They listen well and solicit input into their decision-making. Such people demonstrate care and empathy and express praise to others for a job well done.

4. **Dependability** reflects the fact that you do what you say that you will do. This means keeping promises and commitments. It also includes being punctual, consistent, and responsive.

James Davis, professor of strategic management and the chairman of the Management Department at Utah State University, speaks about three drivers of trust,[42] two of which differ in some way from Olmstead.

> *People in high-trust relationships communicate well, don't second-guess one another, understand why they are doing things, and are willing to go the extra mile to ensure that goals are met.*

1. **Ability**. Can you do what you say you can do? This is similar to Olmstead's first trust element above.

2. **Benevolence**. Do you care about me? Trusted leaders are not ego-driven, but want to do good for others. (This is also called "low self-orientation.") People who are capable but lack benevolence may do all sorts of incredible things, but only if it serves their benefit.

3. **Integrity**. Davis' definition of integrity focuses on shared values. Are the other person's values those that I can agree with? Can I relate to that person because they believe what I believe? (Leadership expert Simon Sinek agrees with this component, adding that "our very survival depends on" our ability to make connections with like-minded others.[43])

---

[41] Blanchard, Kenneth H., Cynthia Olmstead, and Martha C. Lawrence. *Trust Works! Four Keys to Building Lasting Relationships*. New York: William Morrow, 2013.

[42] *Building Trust*. Performed by James Davis. TED Talks. December 6, 2014. Accessed February 22, 2017. https://youtu.be/s9FBK4eprmA.

[43] *First Why and Then Trust*. Performed by Simon Sinek. TED Talks. April 6, 2011. Accessed February 22, 2017. https://youtu.be/4VdO7LuoBzM.

So now we have at least some sense of how to define trust and to help leaders understand its components. But is trust as simple as "if you build it they will come"? After all, aren't there leaders out there who, despite proficiencies in the areas above, still have difficulty earning others' trust and building a trusting work environment?

Perhaps the way to ensure a trusting work environment lies on the other side of the equation. Trust cannot exist in a vacuum. It is a bilateral relationship that requires two to tango. According to Davis, for trust to exist, others must *choose* to make themselves vulnerable to their leaders by taking risks at his behest. And that can be very difficult. In the words of Isaac Watts, quoted in Sinek's TED Talk, "Learning to trust is one of life's most difficult tasks."

One way that leaders can help to increase trust and reduce the defensive posturing that is all too often found in today's organizations is to create a culture that encourages risk-taking. Risks are easier to take when there is less at stake. If I err in good faith and am encouraged to try again, the odds are that I will. If I offer my opinion at a team meeting and my views are respected regardless of their ultimate acceptance, then I will likelier pipe up the next time. If, however, I learn that I am not valued and that winning is the ultimate prize, then I begin to think less about trying something new and different and instead focus on self-preservation. "Don't rock the boat," I tell myself, "and everything will just be fine." Such thinking may produce reliable workers, but it will diminish trust, stunt growth, and encourage people to spend time covering their own backs.

Blaine Lee, a founder of the Covey Leadership Center, expressed this dynamic as follows: "When people honor each other, there is a trust established that leads to synergy, interdependence, and deep respect. Both parties make decisions and choices based on what is right, what is best, what is valued most highly."[44] This, in turn, leads to a happy, productive workplace that is sure to handle all obstacles and market changes in ways that continually move the organization forward.

---

[44] Quoted in Brecher, Natalie D. *Profit from the Power of Many: How to Use Mastermind Teams to Create Success*. Redondo Beach, CA: Cheetah Express, 2004: 37.

CHAPTER 28

Think Positive and Achieve

*If you think you are beaten, you are...If you want
to win, but think you can't, it's almost a cinch you
won't... Success begins with a fellow's will...The man
who wins is the man who thinks he can.*

WALTER D. WINTLE

∼

When Ford CEO Alan Mulally was president at Boeing, it was widely expected that he would be made CEO of the airplane manufacturer. After all, he had presided over a decade of successes at the company, including shepherding Boeing through a vibrant recovery following the heavy impact of 9/11. Understandably, Mulally was devastated when the company passed him over for the top job. But he refused to harp on the negative, because, as he said, "a bad attitude simply erases everyone else's memory of the incredible progress achieved." Why become "the bitter guy" and tarnish his great progress, he thought, when he could remain in everyone's eyes as a proud, successful leader? He took the high road and was promptly recruited by Ford to reignite the massive automobile manufacturer.

∼

One of the biggest challenges for leaders, particularly newer ones, is to remain positive in the face of inevitable setbacks. Leaders who begin with great optimism and energy could easily lose the wind from their sails and spiral into a downward funk when they start to experience obstacles and the self-doubt that accompanies them. Compounding matters is the fact that many of us can be overly harsh and unjust to ourselves, in a way that we would never be with others; this can cause stress and despondency, resulting in lower self-confidence.

One way that leaders can keep their heads up is to engage in positive thinking. This means that you believe that the best is going to happen in every situation rather than the worst. Positive thinking helps you to approach unpleasantness in a more productive way and deal with the things that must be attended to so that you can move forward as quickly as possible.

Positive thinking is not naiveté. Neither does it suggest that you keep your head in the sand and ignore life's less pleasant situations. It simply expresses the belief that you will find a way forward in every situation in a manner that is most healthy and productive.

This may sound simple enough, but for many of us, this can be difficult to implement. Many folks are inclined to see their glasses as half-empty. For them, the optimism and positive press that accompanied them on their way in will not sustain their attitudes and energy levels for very long unless they can find a way to adjust their thinking.

How can we remain positive in the face of adversity? Start by identifying and challenging your negative thoughts. Say, for example, you pinpoint the following concerns:

- Feeling that you are not fully prepared for this position

- Worried about how others will react to your processes, decisions, and/or change initiatives

- A lurking anxiety that things outside your control will undermine your efforts

Now, ask yourself whether each one is reasonable and stands up to a deeper analysis. Let's practice this using the above list.

- **Preparation.** Look yourself in the mirror and ask whether you have trained thoroughly for this position, in your schooling, and through your professional experiences. If you answered "yes," you should be just fine.

- **Others' reactions.** People will respond favorably if they feel that you are well prepared, that you listened well to their thoughts and concerns, and that you made your best efforts to succeed. Do the right things in advance and be confident that your people will support you.

- **What about the things that I can't control?** No leader can fully plan for every eventuality. If you've done contingency planning and considered common risks, however, you should be well prepared for what's to come.

> *Positive thinking is not naiveté. Neither does it suggest that you keep your head in the sand and ignore life's less pleasant situations.*

Fears can easily grip us at moments of uncertainty. When you challenge your fears through careful, rational analysis, it becomes much easier to isolate the real issues and determine whether there is any merit to your fear. Where there is, take appropriate action. Otherwise, rest easy knowing that you've done everything you can to be successful.

Here are some other strategies that can help us think and behave in a more positive and optimistic way:

- **Embrace a healthier lifestyle.** Regular exercise can positively affect mood and reduce stress. Maintain a healthy diet to fuel your mind and body.

- **Become more self-aware.** Intermittently throughout the day, stop and evaluate what you're thinking. Keep notes over a two-week period to see what kind of trends you can identify.

- **Take it slow.** If you see that you are not as optimistic as you would like to be, start small by focusing on one area to approach in a more positive way.

- **Laugh it off.** Stress can make us tighten up and hunker down. Laughing has the opposite effect. It loosens us and allows us to let go and see things for what they really are. To quote Lord Byron, "Always laugh when you can. It is cheap medicine."

- **Surround yourself with positive people.** Make sure those in your life are positive, supportive people. Their energy is contagious, and their sunny outlook will change the way that you look at things. Negative people feed your anxieties and stress levels. They may also make you doubt your ability to succeed.

SECTION 6

MANAGING
CHANGE

CHAPTER 29

Handle Change with Care

Progress is a nice word. But change is its motivator. And change has its enemies.

ROBERT KENNEDY

~

I remember the conversation like it was yesterday. I was on the phone with a veteran principal—a man who was considered one of the more accomplished administrators within the school network to which I belonged. He had agreed to mentor me during my first year as head of school, and he said something at that time that I will never forget.

I can't recall the context that led to the comment. We may have been discussing some of my early challenges. At some point, the conversation shifted to the added burden that I carried in assuming the headship following a decorated, beloved principal.

It was then that my mentor mentioned something about a refund policy common within the recruitment industry. He claimed that when headhunters place a new administrative candidate, they often offer some form of refund if the candidate leaves or is fired soon after that. When the candidate is replacing someone who occupied the position for five years or more, however, then no refund is offered, because the assumption is that things very well may not work out. (In case you're wondering, my mentor was trying to be supportive when he mentioned this by underscoring the challenges of succeeding an established predecessor.)

The fundamental concept behind this policy is that organizational change, represented in the form of new administrative personnel or a different way of operating, can be difficult for all stakeholders. When someone occupies a leadership position for many years, people around the leader adjust to his style and expectations. The leader develops a comfort zone and maintains a basic sense of stability and equilibrium. A new leader represents change, something different and foreign, regardless of his or her core leadership capacity. And that produces anxiety and much nostalgic reflection.

～

Of course, new leaders have no control over prior circumstances or who their predecessors were. Nor do they typically get to choose their administrative team and staff, at least initially. Most new leaders must accept their position with the expectation that they will work with and direct holdover personnel as they advance the organizational mission. This makes it all the more important that they carefully determine when and how they introduce change while deciding on which aspects of organizational function to address first.

Too often, leaders do not appreciate the impact that change can have on an organization. Most people do not like it, even when the suggestion makes sense on paper. This is principally true when such change threatens their status quo, demands that they learn new skills, and/or engage in new work.

While we know that change is critical for organizations, the fact is that it is hard on individuals and teams. Change messes with our routines, raises questions about proper procedure and protocol, and forces us to modify our behaviors. Worst of all, it creates a fundamental baseline of uncertainty that causes many to descend into fear and doubt.

One critical factor in the success of a change initiative is how people feel about the person leading it. John C. Maxwell wrote, "You can't separate the leader from the cause he promotes. It can't be done, no matter how hard you try. It is not an either/or proposition. The two always go together."[45] The first thing your people will see when you introduce change is *you*. If they like what they see and feel that you have taken the time to connect with and understand them, then the process you promote will move forward with much greater ease.

In a similar vein, PricewaterhouseCoopers suggests that change efforts flop when leaders do not create the necessary groundswell of support among their employees.[46] Included in this is their failure to bring employees into

[45] "The Law of Buy-In." Horeb International. N.p., 11 Oct. 2012. Web. 22 Feb. 2017. http://www.horebinternational.com/the-law-of-buy-in/

the conversation in a manner that makes them feel valued and a critical component of the project's success.

We have repeatedly spoken above about the importance of being a good listener. We've noted how leaders who listen can create trustworthy relationships with teammates that are transparent and breed loyalty. Nowhere is this more important than when considering change.

> *A new leader represents change, something different and foreign, regardless of his or her core leadership capacity. And that produces anxiety and much nostalgic reflection.*

Leaders should take steps to elicit genuine feedback, such as by having coffee with small focus groups or by distributing questionnaires to larger workforces. Leaders who do this find that they are better informed of what people are thinking and how they may respond when change is introduced. They can also learn more about personal passions, which may be useful when considering role and committee assignments. The next step is to share what you learned so that you can make the case that the change was driven by them and their feedback, and not by some outside driver.

Change guru John P. Kotter has written that 70 percent of change initiatives in organizations and businesses do not succeed (completely or in part). Kotter outlines eight reasons for such failure, including leaders not establishing a sense of urgency, not developing a vision for change, and/or not effectively communicating their vision.[47]

Citing research from Richard Beckhard and David Gleicher, leadership consultant Deborah Mackin suggests that leaders would also be well served to create a strong case for change together with their primary stakeholders. This increases buy-in and mitigates fears of future second-guessing. As part of the case, Mackin suggests that stakeholders consider the following questions:[48]

---

[46] Paula, Ramona. "PwC Internal Change Capability." Scribd. Accessed February 22, 2017. https://www.pwc.com/us/en/people-management/publications/assets/pwc-internal-change-capability.pdf

[47] Kotter, John P. Leading Change. Boston, MA: Harvard Business School Press, 1996.

[48] "Change Management: Why 70% of Change Initiatives Fail." New Directions Consulting. Accessed February 22, 2017. http://newdirectionsconsulting.com/4639/blog/why-70-of-change-initiatives-fail-2/

1. What is the background for the change?

2. What challenges or problems do we face in the current situation that will cripple us if we don't begin addressing them today?

3. What will the change require?

4. What will it cost us to change?

5. What are we going to have to let go of and why?

6. How will we know when we have succeeded?

By engaging in an honest, comprehensive process that looks at all angles associated with the desired change, leaders can gain greater clarity about the risks and rewards associated with their objectives. Such planning will allow them to craft a more compelling vision that they can sell to others within the organization—a vision that takes others' thoughts and fears into consideration. Most importantly, the outcome of such an honest, thoughtful process will reveal that the leader's agenda is really the organizational agenda—a necessary, consensus-driven process that will provide benefit for the collective enterprise.

Of course, there are exceptions to every rule. Leaders may walk into an urgent situation—such as when the company's outdated thinking and practices threaten its future viability, or when some of its employees are simply not up to the job. In such instances, it is common for leaders to hold out hope that the situation will somehow get better. In most cases, it won't, and you will lose precious credibility along the way for having been unable to recognize the gravity of the problem sooner.

CHAPTER 30

Know When to Shift into (Change) Overdrive

Change is hard because people overestimate the value of what they have—and underestimate the value of what they may gain by giving that up.

JAMES BELASCO AND RALPH STAYER

One quality that separates great chefs from the rest is their ability to be patient. Top culinary artists resist the temptation to stir rice while they're steaming it or to flip steaks unnecessarily. They know when to stir things up and when to let them simmer.

The same can be said for leaders. Great leaders know when to leave things alone and when to stir the pot. Bad leaders, in contrast, like to make change just so that they can get the feeling that they're accomplishing something.

Once you decide that the time is right to make a change, consider these principles to help ensure a smooth, successful process.

- **Don't go it alone.** Never approach change as one man's endeavor, no matter how powerful and supported you may feel. Instead, assemble a group of invested stakeholders with the right combination of power, insight, and collaboration to help you craft and lead the change effort.

- **Maintain low anxiety levels.** Change leaders are effective in fashioning trusting environments where employees feel secure in their jobs and rankings within the organization. Directional or procedural change cannot be presented as a referendum on their capacity as workers, but as a way with which to adjust to market conditions and enhance production. Leaders must also project calm and resolve, no matter what the situation, so that they lead their teams to a better place without unnerving them.

- **Keep it slow and simple at first.** Start slowly if you can. See if there is an area within the organization where you can make soft inroads and study their impact. This will give you meaningful insight into how future, larger launches may be embraced or resisted. Successful change initiatives will also give you an opportunity to rack up a few early wins.

Great leaders know when to leave things alone and when to stir the pot. Bad leaders, in contrast, like to make change just so that they can get the feeling that they're accomplishing something.

- **Roll up your sleeves.** Effective leaders are inclined to step up and participate in the action. They feel energized and exhilarated by the work and the progress. More importantly, employees prefer to engage in new, challenging work if their leaders are leading the way and chipping in.

- **Communicate a clear vision.** Make sure that as many people as possible understand the vision and strategy and how the two connect. The vision must be referred to often, in clear and simple terms that are vivid and easily repeatable, within and without the organization. Include it in company e-mails, meetings, presentations, etc. It should be communicated anywhere and everywhere.

- **Have confidence in your efforts.** For change to happen effectively, people must hold the belief that, despite the unknown risks, the outcomes will be positive and well worth it. In other words, they must be confident in their ability to succeed. Much of that confidence will come through your teaching, direction and continued encouragement, as well as the clear, successful portrait that you paint for them.

It can be tempting for leaders who moved over from a different company to reference previous experiences elsewhere. They have seen such initiatives succeed in other contexts, which gives them the confidence that it'll work in their new company as well. While this may give your new initiative more credibility, be mindful about how you frame it.

When I assumed my principal post, I had relocated from a different city. I often referenced that city and how we had done things over there. My goal was to use that experience to persuade others to my way of thinking. After all, it had worked over there; why wouldn't you see the value of adopting similar practices?

But my approach was fundamentally flawed. Not only was I trying to force an issue based on my own way (or previous community's way) of doing things (as opposed to what was best for my new school community), but I continually framed my arguments as such. "When I was at [my previous school community]," I would say, "we used to _____." That was a big no-no and got me into quite a bit of trouble.

Besides the obvious fact that each work environment is different and that what worked in one situation may not work in another, no one whom you lead wants to hear you say that your previous work environment was superior to your new one. They want to know that you are with them now and are proud to be heading your new institution.

This doesn't mean that you can't reference past experiences or successes. I am simply saying that they should be mentioned in a manner that leads people to conclude that your primary consideration is to enhance the current situation, not to put others down for thinking or acting inferiorly to your previous colleagues. Keep in mind that despite any unique experience and advanced skills that you offer, you remain the newest person on the payroll. You still have to work your way in and earn others' respect.

CHAPTER 31

Enthuse Your Way to Employee Buy-In

A true leader is a person whose influence inspires people to do what is expected of them to do. You cease to be a leader when you manipulate with your egos instead of convincing by your inspirations.

ISRAELMORE AYIVOR

~

A primary challenge for leaders is how to ensure that their employees work diligently, and, where necessary, go the extra mile to meet tight deadlines. To do so, they often bulldoze their agenda through, or, at the most, appeal to the employee's reason and/or emotion. The conversation may sound something like this, depending on the tactic that they employ:

- *Antagonistic*: "There's no choice in the matter. This *must* get done by 5:00 p.m."

- *Sympathetic*: "I feel bad, but I have no choice on this one."

- *Apologetic*: "I'm sorry that I have to drop this on you last-second."

- *Validating*: "I know it's not easy, but it needs to be finished today."

Needless to say, the antagonistic approach is to be avoided whenever possible. Expressions of sympathy or apology may give the worker a feeling of being understood, but they do not engender positive feelings concerning the actual work. The same holds true for validation. You may have acknowledged the employee's feelings, but the lingering tone is still one of burden and imposition.

Instead of looking at the glass as being half-empty, supervisors should consider using an enthusiastic, affirming approach. Try something like: "You are just the one who can save us from our predicament! We're up against a deadline, and this job must get done today. I think that you'd be the best person to get it out accurately and on schedule."

Imagine the difference! The first set of approaches operate from assumptions that the boss can demand whatever he wants (antagonistic), doesn't have the right to make the ask (apologetic), or at least regrets having to do so and appreciates the employee's feelings (sympathetic/validating).

In contrast, by taking the glass-half-full approach, a boss can positively impact internal attitudes and morale. Employees begin to feel valued for their unique talents. They start to see how they can make a particular difference in the organization. Not only will they accept the present work more readily, but they will develop more positive attitudes towards their own self-efficacy and their role within the organization. Hey, they may even volunteer to step up in the future at crunch time!

> *Instead of looking at the glass as being half-empty, supervisors should consider using an enthusiastic, affirming approach.*

Of course, this enthusiastic approach must be used with moderation. Overuse can easily and quickly lead to skepticism and feelings of being taken advantage of. Employers and managers who use this tactic judiciously and make a compelling case as to why this particular employee is most suitable for the job at hand can develop within their staff many of the positive qualities outlined above.

CHAPTER 32

Confront without the Confrontation

To disagree, one doesn't have to be disagreeable.
BARRY GOLDWATER

~

Few leaders can avoid confrontation. There are simply too many employees and functions that require oversight and guidance. The likelihood is very high that a leader will need to address numerous areas of concern within her organization at various points.

Whether the matter is personal (a coworker's attitude or manners, for example) or performance-related, confronting someone can be one of the hardest things for a leader to do. It is unpleasant for leaders to have to bring a concern forward and demand change and improvement. In fact, many leaders will go to extreme lengths to avoid it. Some reasons for this include:

- Fear of how their relationship will be affected moving forward

- Concern over being seen as overly demanding or callous

- Bad feelings from past confrontations that went awry

- Second-guessing and self-doubt regarding their grounds and motives for the confrontation

We also know what can happen when a leader fails to step up and deal with a troubling situation. Without a doubt, it would be a mistake to allow it to continue in the spirit of being a nice guy and hoping that the situation will magically be resolved on its own. Problem behaviors and poor performance need to be addressed early on, and in a clear and firm manner. Doing so will not only help you reset expectations but may also help you understand why the problems are occurring. Your actions will also be appreciated by the rest of your staff, who may be even more fed up with such negativity and mediocrity than you are.

To be clear, the confrontation that we are discussing is not of the aggressive, agitated variety. Such approaches are almost guaranteed to engender ill will and may even go sideways on you. Rather, leaders need to find ways to discuss their concerns in a calm, direct, and proactive fashion. Engaging in productive confrontation paves the way for alternative perspectives, healthier boundaries, innovative approaches, and challenges to the status quo, all of which are essential if we want to enhance our present realities.

Even with a calm presentation, it can be very difficult for leaders to confront others, for the reasons stated above. What can leaders do to overcome their concerns and be more willing to address problems head-on?

1. **Be prepared.** Take the time to assess the situation as fully as possible. This includes understanding the concern thoroughly, in addition to how it impacts you and the company, practically as well as emotionally. Try to separate out the less crucial components from the core considerations. Once you have that clear, prepare for what you will say in detail. In that process, seek to identify the other person's agenda and what her likely reaction will be. Use logic rather than emotion to frame your argument; if you're too worked up emotionally, then you're not ready to move forward. Lastly, seek to identify what an ideal outcome would look like that brings success and satisfaction to you both.

2. **Ask yourself, "How would I want to be approached?"** Often, the best measure for how to advance an unpleasant conversation is to determine how you would like to be approached in such a situation. Unless you are one of those people who let things slide off of your back easily, your intuition should guide you well. Naturally, setting and context are important. No one wants to be confronted in public or while they're in the middle of an important task. Ideally, they should know that the conversation is coming beforehand; this will help them begin to reflect about what might be bothering you.

3. **Stay in control.** Never begin any conversation if you are not in full control of your emotions. If you are not sure that you are ready to manage your emotions before the confrontation, role-play it with

someone you trust and ask for feedback. Practice makes perfect, especially in cases such as these.

4. **Keep the conversation issues-oriented.** There is nothing wrong with being hard on the issues, so long as you remain soft on the person. Affirm your relationship with her and express your commitment to doing what you can to help achieve a positive outcome. Also, express what is

> *Engaging in productive confrontation paves the way for alternative perspectives, healthier boundaries, innovative approaches, and challenges to the status quo, all of which are essential if we want to enhance our present realities.*

working before hitting home on the concerns. When expressing the problems, demonstrate as much care, respect, and compassion as you can muster. Once you have completed your opening statement, stop talking. Don't hedge, qualify, or compromise what you have said. Let the other person respond, and seek to listen. Do your best not to argue. Stay calm, centered, and focused.

5. **Be open to a new outcome.** Though you will spend time thinking about your desired outcome and then rehearsing how to achieve it, it pays to remain open to the possibility of arriving at a different solution. Explore and discuss potential solutions and alternatives, and try to focus on both parties' individual needs and wants.

6. **Set a course of action.** Once you have arrived at an agreement, decide on a follow-up plan. What will each person do to address the issue? Make sure that the goals that you set are S.M.A.R.T. (specific, measurable, achievable, realistic, and timely) and come with an attached timeframe. Then make every effort to stay to the agreed to process.

CHAPTER 33

Learn How to Delegate

*The first rule of management is delegation. Don't try
and do everything yourself because you can't.*

ANTHEA TURNER

~

Sometimes, failure can turn out to be the greatest blessing.

As a young man, Charles Schwab, the founder, chairman, and CEO of
Charles Schwab Corporation, flunked English and was nearly thrown out
of college. He was humiliated because, in his words, he "had always thought
(of himself as a) reasonably smart guy."[49] (Schwab's reading and writing
troubles, he would later discover, were, and still are, the result of dyslexia.)

To address his challenges and meet the demands of his schooling, Schwab
recruited friends and family to help him. "It might seem odd," he later
reflected, "but what felt like a deficit (turned out to be) a real benefit."
Schwab's reading disability taught him how to recruit a talented, trustworthy
team and forced him to become a skilled delegator. Ultimately, those skills
enabled him to scale a business much sooner than most of his classmates at
Stanford Business School. "Brilliant entrepreneurs," he said, "think they can
do everything. They don't spend enough time finding the right people to
grow the business."

~

A few years back I was in attendance at a large convention for educators. A
part of the program that I particularly enjoyed was the full day preconvention
session for school administrators. The speaker that year, a leadership
consultant, created quite a stir when he said (and then continually repeated)

---

[49] Thompson, Mark. "How Top Leaders Handle Setbacks and Criticism." Inc.com. June 06, 2014. Accessed
February 22, 2017. http://www.inc.com/mark-thompson/how-to-survive-criticism.html.

that school administrators should spend very little time in their offices. They should be out and about, he argued, visible and in classrooms, serving in their primary capacity of an instructional leader. The rest of their job, as in the components that did not demand their advanced skills and expertise, could be handled by an effective team of secretaries and support staff.

While his position was repeatedly challenged by numerous principals, who could not see the practicality of his message (it flew in the face of all conventional administrative wisdom), everyone agreed that his words contained some deep truths. It certainly got me thinking about how I could better use my time. In particular, I tried to figure out where my skills and experience would best be directed while delegating to others tasks that I did not need to be dealing with directly, such as scheduling meetings, drafting memos, reviewing curricula, and the like.

Delegation offers many benefits to managers, direct reports, and organizations. Yet it remains one of the most misunderstood and underutilized techniques in leadership practice.

I frequently deliver leadership seminars to executives on the topic of delegation. As part of my talk, I ask participants whether they delegate as much as they should. The majority typically respond to the negative, so I probe further. Using a brainstorming technique, participants are asked to complete the following sentence: "I would delegate more if I…" The following responses are typical:

1. Trusted my colleagues more
2. Wasn't so controlling
3. Had more time to think about what to delegate
4. Knew how

This feedback is not surprising. It is common knowledge that leaders frequently struggle when it comes to relinquishing control and delegating tasks to their associates and direct reports. Why is this so? For one, delegation is a foreign, uncomfortable concept for those who think that they need to hold all of the cards or to have their spoons mixing in every pot. Those who are willing to share responsibility may not invest the time into doing so strategically or may not even know how to go about it at all. Some think that it's simply more efficient for them just to do it themselves.

We all agree that we cannot do it all alone and admit that delegation can help us become much more efficient and effective. So how can leaders utilize delegation more regularly and effectively to help them achieve their goals? Consider following these important steps.

- **Decide what to delegate.** Start with a small project or one that doesn't have to be completed in a specific way. This keeps the temperature low and the end goal in sight.

- **Pick the right person or group.** Take time to understand the strengths and weaknesses of the members of your team. Select those who you're confident can do the job well. They should be self-motivated and comfortable working without constant supervision.

- **Provide adequate training.** Even when you have the right people for the job, you may still need to offer them training to build their skill and efficacy, particularly when the work is new for them. Work with them to figure that piece out to ensure that they feel ready to assume this responsibility.

- **Offer clarity about the expected outcome.** Include timelines and deliverables and provide a template or guidelines for the project. The more that you can spell out, in detail, about what a strong outcome looks like, the less the risk of subsequent confusion or error.

- **Grant the necessary authority.** Supply the control and leeway for your coworker to find the best approach on his own. This increases his creativity and initiative while boosting his self-esteem.

- **Learn to trust your team.** Trust is the single most crucial element to effective delegation and teamwork. You have to believe in your people to empower them. Theodore Roosevelt once said, "The best executive is one who has sense enough to pick good people to do what he wants done, and self-restraint enough to keep from meddling with them while they do it."

- **Be prepared to assist.** You may need to delegate the task as a whole, but can often still assist here or there. This can be a bit tricky. Many leaders want to avoid micromanagement and feel that once they delegate, they need to step back and give over the reins. But a hands-off management style isn't a very good idea. You need to get the balance right.

- **Monitor progress.** Stay on top of things, and correct/redirect when necessary. This motivates colleagues (who don't feel abandoned) and helps you catch problems early. Obviously, inexperienced colleagues will need tighter control and oversight than seasoned ones.

- **Recognize key milestones and celebrate successes.** Anything from a simple "thank you" or "well done" to arranging for awards, gifts or bonuses.

- **Create a delegation culture.** Give your direct reports permission to remind you when you haven't delegated something that you should. No one wants to be viewed as criticizing the boss, so emphasize that you are open to and expect this kind of input. Also, make clear to others that if they see a project they want to take on, they should ask for it.

The process of building a well-informed and properly trained team allows leaders to harness various talents and perspectives for the collective good. It may be challenging at first but will pay great dividends over time while also alleviating some of the crushing burdens that often sit on a leader's shoulders.

For those who prefer formulas, you may want to consider leadership expert John C. Maxwell's 10-80-10 rule.[50] He divides delegated projects into three segments: the first 10 percent, the middle 80 percent, and the last 10 percent. Maxwell involves himself in the first and last 10 percent while the middle work is carried by his team, as detailed below.

Maxwell compares his involvement, which he calls "the bookends of success," to the process of piloting a plane. The crucial parts of the flight— the most dangerous and complicated—are takeoff and landing. These are the components that most need a leader's input and attention. The rest of the "flight" is doable by his team.

---

[50] John Maxwell, "The 10-80-10 Principle: The Key To Maximizing Your Time and Effort," *John Maxwell on Leadership* (blog), July 22, 2014, http://www.johnmaxell.com/blog/the-10-80-10-principle-the-key-to-maximizing-your-time-and-effort

During the first 10 percent of the delegation process, Maxwell provides his team with the following so that they can complete their primary tasks (the middle 80 percent):

- **The big picture.** As a leader, you often see more than others do. Maxwell uses this time to share his big picture vision and discuss outcomes.

- **Objectives.** Following the initial vision, Maxwell works to break down the goal into specific objectives, typically limiting the number to four or five. These help those involved understand the "how" of the process: as in, "how are we going to achieve the overarching goal?" The simpler the objectives, and the more visual they are made, the easier it'll be for your team to be able to look at them later and know whether they're still on target.

- **Direction.** After the objectives have been set, it's important for each team member to know his or her specific responsibilities. This helps to maximize efforts, increase accountability, and avoid conflict.

- **Resources and support.** This is similar to what we discussed above. What do they need, in terms of resources and assistance, to make it work?

> *The crucial parts of the flight—the most dangerous and complicated—are takeoff and landing. These are the components that most need a leader's input and attention. The rest of the "flight" is doable by his team.*

At the end of each delegated project, Maxwell listens to a full progress report. He then uses his experience to ask the kinds of questions that will determine what holes exist in the present process and shares insights about how best to move things forward to completion.

As you can see, delegation is far from a simple process. That's one key reason as to why so many folks that should be delegating more fail to do so. By following these steps, leaders can become more conscientious of the need to delegate and better equip others in their workplace to assume responsibility with skill and confidence.

SECTION 7

GET THE
WORKPLACE
HUMMING

CHAPTER 34

Prioritize a Passionate Workplace

If a man is called to be a street sweeper, he should sweep streets even as Michelangelo painted, or Beethoven composed music, or Shakespeare wrote poetry. He should sweep streets so well that all the hosts of heaven and earth will pause to say, "here lived a great street sweeper who did his job well."

DR. MARTIN LUTHER KING, JR.

~

The staff that I inherited as head of school included a wonderfully talented office administrator, who we'll call Laurie. Laurie served as my personal secretary and was the glue that held the front office together. Here and there, this woman also handled student registration and performed some admissions-related functions that were not officially part of her job description. Laurie did all of her tasks well and with good cheer.

As time moved on, I felt that we were wasting many of Laurie's talents. Many of the secretarial functions could be reassigned, leaving her with more time to focus on the more sophisticated and engaging tasks that our school needed and that she craved. So, I promoted her to a newly-created post of Admissions Director, while also making Laurie the lead person in the areas of PR and multimedia.

It became a huge win-win. Laurie received a promotion and a slight salary increase to do a job that she was passionate about and genuinely enjoyed. The school received increased passion (including a willingness to work longer hours) and a real boost in areas where we had been long deficient. Even now, years later, I get occasional notes from Laurie, thanking me for believing in her abilities and giving her the chance to shine (and have more fun at work).

~

It is well-documented that many folks are not passionate about their work. According to a White Paper by Deloitte University Press,[51] up to 87.7 percent of America's workforce does not contribute to their full potential because they don't have passion for their work.

At the beginning of *StrengthsFinder 2.0,*[52] Tom Rath presents some equally disheartening data. He relates that Gallup had surveyed more than ten million people worldwide on the topic of employee engagement. In that survey, only one third strongly agreed with the following statement: "At work, I have the opportunity to do what I do best every day." In a related poll of 1000 participants, all of whom responded that they disagree or strongly disagree with the above statement ("At work..."), not a single one said that they were emotionally engaged at work.

It is important to note that the terms "passion" and "engagement" are often used interchangeably when referring to employee work attitude and effort. Many experts point out, however, that passion is the goal because it expresses a long-term, intrinsic motivation to work at a high level. Engagement, on the other hand, can be shorter-term in nature and often speaks to extrinsic motivators (such as praise, competition, incentives and the like) that push folks who normally assume a passive (or worse) posture to "get into it" for a period.

In today's rapidly changing business environment companies need passionate workers because such workers can drive extreme and sustained performance improvement—more than the one-time performance bump that often follows a bonus or the implementation of a worker engagement initiative. Passionate workers also possess personal resilience and an orientation toward learning. This can be particularly helpful for companies that need to withstand continuous market challenges and disruptions.

What does a passionate employee look like? According to Deloitte, such workers (among other things):

- Bring noticeable energy to their work

---

[51] "Passion at Work." DU Press. Accessed February 22, 2017. http://dupress.com/articles/worker-passion-employee-behavior/.

[52] Rath, Tom. *Strengths Finder 2.0.* New York: Gallup Press, 2007: ii-iii.

- Search for new, better solutions to challenging problems
- Takes meaningful risks to improve performance
- Cut across silos to deliver results
- Are happier to go to work each day, which translates to less sick time off
- Are more loyal to their employers
- Work as needed to get the job done, and, perhaps most important
- Perform at a higher level with each passing year

In addition to the above, passionate *teams*:

- Inspire others around them, because passion begets passion
- More willingly create a team-oriented atmosphere

Since we know that such passion does not grow on trees, it's important for employers and team leaders to give serious consideration to the question of how can we increase it among our employees. The following strategies can be helpful for leaders who want to instill more passion into their workplace:

- **Make it a priority.** Look for passion at every step, particularly at the beginning. Include questions about passion in the interview process and be willing to prioritize it over experience and credentials to find people who share your passions and interests. Ask such questions as: What do you love about your chosen career? What inspires you? What kind of work or subjects do you dread? How to you feel about working with others and taking risks? You want to get a sense of what the potential employee *feels* and *believes*.

This is not to say that experience and credentials are not important. But with so many high-quality CVs typically at their disposal, employers can afford to use passion as a driving/determining element in their decision on who to hire.

- **Connect to their emotions.** Passion is an emotion, a state of mind. While many leaders may think task-first and seek to leave their emotions out of things, this can be damaging to worker passion. Workers need to know that their work matters and see how it all comes together. Encourage them to engage with customers and other ecosystem partners. The more that they feel that they're innovating and making a difference, the better they will typically perform.

- **Break down barriers.** Sometimes the biggest obstacles to passion are barriers that prevent people from making it happen. Silos, real or imagined, exist in almost every workplace, particularly larger entities. By encouraging people to work cross-functionally, you tap into their connecting disposition and keep them from feeling confined, which can drain their passion and sense of possibility.

- **Craft the job around their interests and abilities.** The sign of a good coach is that he or she develops a system and game plan around the players. Teams that have a certain type of personnel do best when they take full advantage of the talent and abilities on the roster. Similarly, team leaders ought to be willing to identify their keepers and then adjust such things as job descriptions and requirements around them. Be flexible where possible to ensure that folks feel that you have their best interests in mind. Also, encourage your people to ask to work on projects they are interested in instead of (or as well as) those to which they are assigned.

> *As leaders, it is our job to find ways to bring that passion out and make it part of how your people think and operate. Make passion and strengths-based management a requirement.*

- **Build their capacity and efficacy.** We discussed this in the chapter about delegation. Offer training and educational opportunities to help your people grow and become more confident in their work. Nothing drives passion like a deep sense of ability and aptitude. Also, encourage your people to connect with others in their industry. This will offer many benefits, including new insights, stronger connections and leads, and, perhaps most important, an outlet for folks when they need advice or someone with whom to talk.

- **Put passion all around them**. Hire great managers and team members who are engaged and passionate about helping others discover their talents. Passion breeds passion.

We're all passionate about certain things. For too many, this passion does not extend to the workplace. As leaders, it is our job to find ways to bring that passion out and make it part of how your people think and operate. Look beyond people's knowledge, talents, and experiences to see what makes them tick and what kind of work will get them going. The more work that is done to develop and trigger workplace passion, the more leaders can expect the kind of productivity and climate that sets companies apart.

CHAPTER 35

Give Your People the Gift of Mentoring

Mentoring is a brain to pick, an ear to listen, and a push in the right direction.

JOHN C. CROSBY

~

One of the most important things that a leader can do for his people is to provide them with mentors. Mentors help others grow in their positions in a way that no training program or job-based experience can.

Strong internal mentoring programs have been found to increase employee job satisfaction and retention. A 2013 study found that employee retention rates in their sample group of mentors and mentees climbed 69 percent for the mentors and 72 percent for the mentees (or protégés) over a seven-year period.[53]

But what exactly does a strong mentoring relationship look like? Without question, it begins with the mentor.

One time I was invited to speak to a group of institutional advancement professionals on the topic of mentorship. There were approximately eighty people in the room, and I told them all to imagine an ideal mentoring arrangement. Using a scaling exercise, I asked them to tell me, in vivid detail, what a "perfect ten" looked and felt like.

The audience listed many attributes of strong mentorship. Some of the qualities were technical, such as being consistent and available, as well as being accountable and following through on commitments. Others talked

---

[53] Ghosh, Rajashi, and Thomas G. Reio. "Career Benefits Associated with Mentoring for Mentors: A Meta-Analysis." *Journal of Vocational Behavior*, vol. 83, no. 1, 2013, pp. 106-116doi:10.1016/j.jvb.2013.03.011.

about mentor attitudes. These included treating mentees as adults, not people to be spoken down to. Another one mentioned was for mentors to be success-oriented, meaning that they are driven by a genuine desire to succeed and see the mentee's success as their own.

The largest bucket was filled with relational qualities, such as being authentic and not trying to put on a show for the mentee as a way of earning respect. To this audience, the best mentor-mentee dynamic is natural and fluid. This comes from the mentor being a good listener and developing trust. Another contributor was the mentor's ability to use their experience to help guide and support the mentee, but in a manner that was guidance-driven rather than imposing solutions.

I had also asked participants to tell me what a one (lowest score) looked and felt like. Mostly, the response sounded like the opposite of a ten. Specifically, some shared that they felt used in bad mentorship pairings; it was as if the mentor was most interested in resume-building instead of the mentee's growth. They also cited feeling a lack of validation.

Superior mentors possess most, if not all, of the following qualities:

- **Skilled and knowledgeable.** Strong mentors possess current and relevant knowledge, expertise, and/or skills. In the study mentioned in chapter 11, researchers found that mentors who had already achieved success in the tech industry were able to help younger tech startups outperform their peers by a factor of three.

- **Role model.** The mentor should be everything that the mentee needs to become, as an employee and as a person. Realize that the mentee will be studying you closely and will draw deeply from your actions and values.

In the 1930s, there was a young boy in India who had become addicted to eating sugar. His mother decided to get help, so she took him on a long journey under the scorching sun to see the great Gandhi.

When she finally reached Gandhi, she asked him to tell her son to stop eating sugar as it wasn't good for his health. Gandhi replied, "I cannot tell him that right now. Bring him back in a few weeks and then I will talk to him." The mother, confused and upset, had no choice but to take the boy home.

Two weeks later she came back. This time Gandhi looked directly at the boy and said, "Son, you should stop eating sugar. It is not good for your health." The boy nodded his head and promised he wouldn't. The boy's mother was puzzled. She asked, "Why didn't you tell him that two weeks ago when I brought him here to see you?" Gandhi smiled and said, "Mother, two weeks ago I was eating a lot of sugar myself."

Some shared that they felt used in bad mentorship pairings; it was as if the mentor was most interested in resume-building instead of the mentee's growth.

Gandhi recognized that he would have no credibility with this child if he did not do what he would ask of the boy. He began to build credibility by personally refraining from eating sugar so that he could make that same request of his visitor.

- **Trust-builder.** A good mentor establishes a high level of trust. He or she indicates that the relationship is about building capacity and offering support, not zapping the mentee for poor decisions or performances.

- **Active listener.** A strong mentor knows how to listen. This includes using eyes and body posture to convey interest and attention.

- **Strong analyst.** Mentors must be able to analyze what needs to get done and then help the mentee create an action plan for success. They also need to be able to see how the mentee's abilities align with the task and help him or her optimize strengths towards that end.

- **Honest, clear communicator.** It is important for mentors to be super-clear about what the job entails as well as what they are observing. Be honest and specific about what is or is not working and use measurable criteria to assess performance.

- **Committed and reliable.** Mentees should know that they can trust their mentor to be there for them and help them through until the very end. On a related note, good mentors are sincerely interested in helping someone else without any formal reward. They do it because they genuinely want to see someone else succeed.

- **Sustained.** Supporting leaders requires consistent contact. Ideally, mentor and mentee should meet at least once each quarter for continued support and direction. It is critical that mentors be willing and able to make a meaningful commitment to their mentee.

- **Cheerleader.** This is perhaps the most important quality of all. Mentors need to be a source of inspiration for their mentees, especially when the pressure to perform mounts. Guidance, coupled with a healthy dose of encouragement, can be the magic formula to ensure a mentee's short- and long-term success.

Mentoring programs typically fail because one or more positive ingredients listed above are missing. As noted above, the mentor's head has to be fully in the game. Also, a mentor has to be able to earn the mentee's trust. That is not as simple as it sounds. In addition to demonstrating capacity, effective mentors find ways to make their mentees genuinely feel that they have the mentee's best interests in mind.

One great way by which to build such trust is to think in terms of abundance. Abundance Theory sees the world as offering infinite possibilities (more on this in chapter 38). It suggests that not only is there plenty to go around (the opposite of scarcity thinking), but also posits that my helping others will help me as well, by sharpening my skill set and building increased capacity and demand within the field.

Mentors who enter relationships with abundance thinking are invariably going to give their mentee everything that they can in terms of time, attention, and advice. They are also likelier to remain committed for more time, to do their share in making sure that progress is being made, and to see that the mentee follows through on his or her end. Perhaps most importantly, such abundance thinking can be felt and sensed by mentees. They come to recognize quickly how invested in their success the mentor is, and they make sure not to disappoint.

Employers can help mentors by creating structured mentor programs with clear, quantifiable goals for both parties. Also, the more they can contribute to the creation of a less competitive work environment that will allow mentors to offer real help without having to worry about time lost from their own responsibilities, the likelier it is that mentors will willingly sign up and make the most of these relationships.

CHAPTER 36

Build a Team of Workplace Teachers

*(As a leader) you must know what you want to achieve, be
certain of your aims, and have these goals constantly in mind...
You must educate your (people)...And since the world never
stops for a moment...you must constantly reassess chosen
policies towards the achievement of your aims.*

DAVID BEN-GURION, FIRST PRIME MINISTER OF ISRAEL

～

One key component of assuming the mantle of leadership—especially for
leaders who were promoted internally—is the role that they'll need to
play as a teacher. Diane Omdahl, president and co-founder of the Medicare
consultation firm 65 Incorporated, said that when she first experienced
this transition, she realized there were many opportunities for teaching
moments. But the challenge often lies in knowing when and how to do so.

～

Much has been written about how twenty-first-century leaders differ from
their twentieth-century counterparts. Today's leaders must guide complex
organizations that are more virtual and multinational in nature than ever
before. They must nimbly navigate through a fast-paced marketplace that is
in continuous flux and determine the proper course forward from a myriad
of options. They also need to recruit and retain a millennial workforce that
has different interests, needs, and working habits than their elders.

In such a demanding business climate, leaders would be wise to develop a
strong learning environment at the workplace. The celebrated CEO of GE,
Jack Welch, famously said, "an organization's ability to learn, and translate

that learning into action rapidly, is the ultimate competitive advantage."[54] Continuous learning and successful implementation of that learning is crucial to the success of today's organizations.

But learning alone is not enough. Leaders who want to stay ahead must make sure that their companies also place a premium on teaching.

To be a learner is to engage in a one-way (receiving) process of understanding, followed by action. The learning originates from an outside source: consultant, seminar presentation, book, etc. Even if the organization chooses to integrate the learning, it never really owns it.

In contrast, teaching organizations go one meaningful step further. They emphasize teaching over learning, placing the learning onus on internal personnel who are expected to learn and grasp ideas that they will then pass along to others in the workplace.

Research clearly shows that we remember more when we teach than when we listen. This is because the need to teach material forces us to master the content, to the point where we can deliver it clearly to others. As my ninth-grade teacher used to say, "If you can't say (or teach) it, then you don't know it."

It may sound all nice and good to add teaching responsibilities to the mix, but we know that most workplaces are not filled with experienced teachers and presenters. How can leaders expect to implement a teaching culture is they don't have a stable of instructors on hand to advance learning?

As a former principal who has observed countless teachers, I can attest that the best teachers are the ones who can make learning clear, interesting, and relevant. This ability stems mainly from a deep quest for personal learning as well as the ability to ask tough questions and present answers in a way that others can to process and understand.

When preparing their talks or meetings, have your "teachers" think in terms of these five *P*s:

    1. Paint a picture. Create a vision of what others will do as the

---

[54] Quoted in Gibbs, Richard, and Andrew Humphries. *Strategic Alliances & Marketing Partnerships: Gaining Competitive Advantage through Collaboration and Partnering*. London: Kogan Page, 2009: 71.

result of this learning/process. Give them something vivid and exciting to wrap their heads around.

2. **Personal.** Let others know what's in it for them by learning this. How will it change and enhance their jobs? How will it help the company grow and become stronger?

3. **Praise.** Encourage learners with lots of praise and recognition of their achievements as well as their willingness to take risks.

4. **Perseverance.** This can be the hardest part for both teacher and pupil. Challenges will invariably arise, particularly after the opening enthusiasm has waned. Be ready to work even harder mid-process so as not to lose steam.

5. **Perform.** It's not enough to share ideas and preach compliance. Good teachers know that they achieve a great deal through modeling. Show them what you want and then "walk the walk." That will do much for your credibility while also reinforcing desired behaviors and thought processes.

> *Research clearly shows that we remember more when we teach than when we listen. This is because the need to teach material forces us to master the content, to the point where we can deliver it clearly to others.*

In summary, I present to you the words of Noel Tichy, author of *The Leadership Engine* and *Cycle of Leadership*: "We have looked at winning companies—those that consistently outperform competitors and reward shareholders—and found that they've moved beyond being learning organizations to become teaching organizations...That's because teaching organizations are more agile, come up with better strategies, and are able to implement them more effectively...Teaching organizations do share with learning organizations the goal that everyone continually acquire new knowledge and skills. But to do that, they add the more critical goal that everyone pass their learning on to others...In a teaching organization, leaders benefit just by preparing to teach others. Because the teachers are people with hands-on experience within the organization—rather than outside consultants—the people being taught learn relevant, immediately useful concepts and skills. Teaching organizations are better able to achieve success and maintain it because their constant focus is on developing people to become leaders." [55, 56]

---

[55] Tichy, Noel M., and Eli B. Cohen. *The Leadership Engine: How Winning Companies Build Leaders at Every Level*. New York, NY: Harper Business, 1997.

[56] Tichy, Noel M., and Eli Cohen. 1998. "The Teaching Organization." *Training & Development* 52 (7): 26.

CHAPTER 37

Foster a Growth Mindset

Get away from these two types of people: the ones who think you can only go as far as the situation you were born into; and the ones who think you can only go as far as the current situation you are in.

DEE DEE M. SCOTT

~

I often find myself having some variation of the following conversation with an organization's chief executive, HR director, or program coordinator in advance of my presentations. "Please make sure," they say, "to include lots of practical examples for everyone in the room when you speak." They explain their request as follows. "Often when we bring someone in to present a workshop we get blowback, particularly from the old-timers. They've told us that other presenters' content was too theoretical. They also say that the examples may have been useful to others in the room, but it did not address their specific needs."

As a former teacher and principal, I know exactly what that person is talking about. So often, I would sit through a workshop and wonder about its applicability to me and my classroom. Many others around me would do similarly, and often find other more useful things to do, such as grade papers. When I became a principal, I found the problem to be even more acute. Body language and feedback forms shared a constant message questioning workshops' relevance, utility, and application.

Naturally, some of this relates to the program's structure. First, organizations that invest minimally in their professional development programming will often invite everyone to a workshop, even when the needs and interests of attendees are very different. If the presenter does not bring the audience to a place where they can discuss, process, share, and make concrete applications to their specific setting and context, it will typically be a long day for all involved. One size can often fit none. Another factor, no doubt, is whether the leader has helped his or her teams understand the importance and utility of the session content.

But I often view this pushback as attitudinal, regardless of the group's composition or the presenter's capacities and engagement techniques. "Don't bother me," they say (or think in their minds), "I know what I'm doing." This is particularly true about the proverbial "old dogs" who don't want to learn new tricks. Of course, no one wants to admit to being closed to new learning. Instead, they attack presentations as being too abstract, without enough "ready-made, special for me" examples that they can bring back to my workspace, with no effort on their part, and use immediately.

Where do such adverse attitudes come from? Is it laziness? Is arrogance at play, suggesting that there is nothing that you can teach me that I don't already know?

> *The job of the leader is to promote awareness of growth capabilities and get people beyond their limiting beliefs. It's not that you can't do it. You just can't do it yet.*

I would say "yes" to both, at least to some degree. Most people won't work harder unless they see a real benefit in doing so. And if past processes have worked, why should they assume that a new way is necessarily better?

I think that there's another factor at play here. In her bestselling book, *Mindset: The New Psychology Of Success,* Stanford professor Carol Dweck discusses people's mindsets with regard to their ability to perform new tasks.[57] She talks about people who stay squarely in their comfort zones and others that venture well beyond them. Dweck labeled these mindsets as "fixed" and "growth," respectively.

A fixed mindset refers to the belief that skill and capacity are fundamentally attached to a person's genetic composition. Either you "have it" and are good at it, or you're not. This applies to everything from academics ("I'm not much of a math guy") to business and social situations ("I don't know marketing"), as well as music, athletics, and more.

---

[57] Dweck, Carol S. *Mindset: The New Psychology of Success.* New York: Random House, 2006.

Those with growth mindsets, on the other hand, tend to believe that skills can be learned, at least to some degree of proficiency. They maintain that success depends mainly on one's willingness to learn, practice, and pursue their goals. These men and women are not content to rest on their laurels and just ride on the coattails of their natural capacities as far as they would take them. Instead, they continuously strive to learn new things and to develop new capabilities. They do so in part because of their great drive to succeed. But they also possess a deep sense that they can stretch their inborn talents if they are willing to make an effort.

Take, for example, Michael Jordan, arguably the best basketball player ever. Jordan was undeniably a gifted athlete. But so were many others who didn't make it to the top of professional basketball's summit. Jordan became the best because he was driven to be the best. No one competed more vigorously and consistently or wanted to win more than he did. But he also was willing to learn, from his coaches and teammates, and work to improve his areas of weakness in order to excel. Effort alone—without the recognition that new skills could be learned—would never have produced the desired outcome.

Most people are not exclusively fixed- or growth-oriented in how they think. We are typically somewhere in between. The farther the task from our comfort zone, however, the more we throw up "disability blocks" that justify our lack of effort to learn.

The job of the leader is to promote awareness of growth capabilities and get people beyond their limiting beliefs. It's not that you can't do it. You just can't do it *yet*.

How can leaders help promote more of a growth mindset at work to ensure that they get the most out of their teams?

- **Start with the interview.** When meeting potential candidates, ask them what they're good at and how they became good in those areas. See what their past challenges were and what they did to overcome them. Ask them how they would approach scenarios that demand more of them than what is in their present comfort zones. If they possess a healthy combination of skill and experience and also demonstrate a growth mindset, you can be confident that you're bringing a lifelong learner into your organization who will add much value to the team.

- **Communicate its importance.** Tell everyone in the organization about growth mindset and why it matters. Tell stories that capture its benefits, such as someone who was stuck and broke through and what that paradigm shift meant for him and his organization.

- **Make the required knowledge and skills available.** It's much easier to demand this of people if you give them the tools to find answers and become better. Build strong libraries and resource centers for easy reference and learning. Develop intranet groups for staff communication and idea-sharing. Identify resident experts who can coach and mentor others.

Leaders who promote growth mindsets at work will find that their team is more learning oriented and adaptive, two crucial qualities of the twenty-first-century worker.

CHAPTER 38

Abundance Theory in the Workplace

*He who wishes to secure the good of others has
already secured his own.*

CONFUCIUS

~

A few years back, I had made the decision to shift careers from school leadership to executive coach and consultant. To that end, I enrolled in a doctoral program studying human and organizational psychology. In my first course, I was told to interview someone who was in the same field that I sought to pursue and ask that person a series of questions relating to their career path.

After doing some research, I found two successful women who fit the bill. While both were pleasant to speak with and generous with their time, one in particular, a coach and trainer, shared some things that made an impression on me. She said that she had benefitted from others' expertise when she had gotten started and was always looking for ways to pay it forward to other aspiring professionals. The fact that I was planning to move to her general area and serve similar clients did not deter her from giving freely of her advice. She even met me on another occasion over lunch to talk further about how to help me transition and grow my business.

This woman's behavior not only helped me to get started but also inspired me to rethink a lifelong script that had become part of my inner thinking and attitude. I refer specifically to Scarcity Theory.

Scarcity Theory, a term coined by Stephen Covey, suggests that everything in life has its limit. Whether that thing is a spot on the team roster, a scholarship, a job, customers, funding, promotions, or something else, we feel the need to hoard as much as possible for ourselves, because there is simply not enough to go around. This same theory also says that there are limited ways to achieve success and that anyone who wishes to make it must follow the same path and prescription that others have done previously.

In contrast, this coach, through her word and deed, demonstrated to me a living illustration of what Covey labeled Abundance Theory (AT). Abundance Theory is a mindset that looks at each glass as half full (if not fuller) and sees the world as offering endless opportunity. To the abundance theorist, there will always be room on the bench for one more player, and that new player will not detract from anybody's ability to earn a livelihood or achieve other professional or personal goals. The world offers plenty; our job is to know how to go out and find it, and then share some of it with others.

Moreover, to the abundance practitioner, the more is often the merrier. Consider coaching, for example. Not only does the presence of more coaches not detract from individual coaches' underlying ability to engage and support sufficient clients, but it also generates added awareness about the importance of coaching as a service and lends credibility to the field by increasing the number of qualified practitioners. In addition, the more minds that are applied to solving issues and creating solutions, the better for everyone. If one coach develops tools that help clients, they can share their successes with others and raise the collective coaching standard for all.

The benefits of abundance thinking extend to leaders as well. Teams and organizations that think "we first" tend to outperform their competition. They are less consumed with internal territorialism and personal recognition and focus instead on finding solutions and improving performance. Abundance thinkers understand that with the victory—measured by their ability to work together and support each other—come the spoils.

Some leaders may find Abundance Theory to be a tough sell. We noted above that most folks have been taught at one point or another that there are finite limits to many of the things that they desire. Leaders, for their part, may have also adopted a scarcity mindset as they moved along their educational and professional pathways. How can they now turn around and preach abundance? The following strategies may help:

- **Describe the merits.** For many, abundance thinking is foreign. For leaders to rewrite their people's thinking, they must list the many benefits of AT, such as the ones listed above.

- **Recognize and reward those who are inclusive.** Leaders should note examples of abundance thinking and action in the workplace and shine attention on it. If they can reinforce it with some form of reward, all the better.

To the abundance theorist, there will always be room on the bench for one more player, and that new player will not detract from anybody's ability to earn a livelihood or achieve other professional or personal goals.

- **Create opportunities for idea-sharing.** Model AT by giving people a chance to provide input and wrap their heads around issues. Emphasize how good ideas from one will benefit the entire group.

- **Remind yourself.** Leaders who are not scripted in AT need to continually remind themselves of it and its implications. When considering options and making decisions, place a reminder squarely in front of you to ensure that you are mindful of it when it matters most.

- **Make it a workplace competency.** As with other job-related qualifications, leaders should look for evidence of AT when hiring new personnel. Certainly, it would be a good quality for team leaders to possess.

- **Give more of what you want.** One of the best ways to increase your abundance is to give. People appreciate generosity and often find ways to give back.

CHAPTER 39

Get the Most out of Meetings

*I find most meetings are a waste of time, because they
are so ill-prepared and there's little opportunity for true
synergy in producing better solutions than what anyone
originally thought of. So I work hard to only attend those
meetings that have strategic importance and miss all kinds
of other seemingly urgent meetings.*

STEPHEN R. COVEY

Meetings get a bad rap, and deservedly so—most are disorganized and distracted. But they can be a critical tool for getting your team on the same page. In the words of Peter Guber, CEO of Mandalay Entertainment Group: "Nothing replaces being in the same room, face-to-face, breathing the same air and reading and feeling each other's micro-expressions."

Where have you seen this before? After a busy morning, staff members gather together in a conference room. For the next hour, they listen to an executive offer a point-to-point review of a litany of technical items including quarterly figures, scheduling, new projects, policies, etc. They sit around passively with limited participation or engagement. Most look at the clock, waiting impatiently for their release.

As a former teacher and administrator, I have sat through or run countless staff meetings. With precious little time for conversation and a wide range of areas to address, these assemblies often took on a rushed, disengaged feeling. The agenda moved quickly from point to point, with little time for processing and input. Even when attendees did weigh in with questions, comments, or opinions, they rarely resulted in meaningful conversation or change in direction. The result was frustration for everyone present and a pained smile on the way out.

After running such meetings for nearly two years, I began to rethink them. My goal was to make them positive, productive, collaborative experiences, not something to avoid. To do that, I changed my approach and scaled back the agenda. Our conversations became more robust. Teachers were given more opportunity to grapple with real issues rather than being inundated with minutia and technicalities.

What changed? First, I cut out as much announcement-type information as possible. Those were distributed by e-mail and/or weekly memos. Of course, "good and welfare" announcements remained, as they gave us the opportunity to celebrate with one another and offer support. But our staff meetings were no longer bogged down by the low-level detail that could be read and reviewed just as easily in advance of the meeting, in a manner that gave teachers the ability to process and offer feedback as warranted.

> *Company and team meetings can be a real drag. They can also be tools for exciting engagement. Your employees are all so busy and deserve to have their time and opinions valued.*

Not surprisingly, our meetings began to take on a real purpose. In previous years, they had felt perfunctory at times, as though we were meeting simply because the calendar told us to. Now, we were meeting with more engaged purpose, usually to discuss the next stage of a strategic priority or professional development objective.

Discussions were structured cooperatively, to ensure that all attendees participated and had a voice. Sometimes this was done in simple think-pair-share format.[58] At other times, cooperative jigsaw groupings were used.[59] By putting teachers into informal committee, we were able to get great feedback on issues that mattered in a manner that was focused, productive, and efficient.

---

[58] "Think, Pair, Share Cooperative Learning Strategy: For Teachers (Grades K-12)." For Teachers (Grades K-12) - TeacherVision. Accessed February 22, 2017. https://www.teachervision.com/group-work/cooperative-learning/48547.html.

[59] "Jigsaw Groups for Cooperative Learning: Teaching Strategy for Students (Grades K-12)." Teaching Strategy for Students (Grades K-12) - TeacherVision. Accessed February 22, 2017. https://www.teachervision.com/group-work/cooperative-learning/48532.html?detoured=1.

As noted above, company and team meetings can be a real drag. They can also be tools for exciting engagement. Your employees are all so busy and deserve to have their time and opinions valued. By creating action-oriented agendas that offer the opportunity to talk, debate, and vote, leaders can transform their meetings from something just slightly better than a trip to the dentist's office to a truly engaging and beneficial experience that may actually get people excited to attend.

CHAPTER 40
Link the Silos

"When we link our office silos, walk over to talk to our colleagues instead of calling, texting, or e-mailing them, allow time for chit-chat and collaborate with other practice groups, pods and departments, our culture is elevated and our clients can feel it."

LEE K. BROEKMAN

∿

I once delivered a talk at an institutional advancement conference on the topic of identifying and communicating a school's unique qualities and mission.[60] During the presentation, an issue emerged that sits at the forefront of the minds of many of the professionals who were in attendance.

I spoke of the need for advancement personnel (development, admissions, recruitment/retention, communications, marketing, etc.) to connect deeply and continually with the academic leadership. Too often, the two offices operate as independent silos, with each group focused almost exclusively on their respective domains, without much awareness or interest in what is occurring across the hallway or elsewhere on campus.

Part of this dynamic may come from each group's familiarity and comfort level. Academic leaders are usually promoted from the classroom. They excel as instructors and instructional leaders and prefer to talk about pedagogy, to engage with teachers and students, and to deal with the kinds of tasks that are typically associated with school function (scheduling, supervision, curriculum, etc.) Advancement personnel, in contrast, may not have any background as educational professionals; a sizable number of participants at my talk came to their current schools from the for-profit world and held degrees that were not education-specific.

---

[60] *Linking Silos: Academic Leadership and Institutional Advancement.* Naphthali Hoff. April 26, 2015. Accessed February 22, 2017. https://youtu.be/e4qJTawMhgw.

As a former principal, I can also speak
to the fact that many school leaders
do not feel all that comfortable, or at
least not all that motivated, to address
advancement-related tasks and support
their colleagues on the other side of
the educational aisle. They see their
jobs as principal teachers (the title
that spawned the term "principal") and
view the business side of institutional

> *Change is a huge challenge for leaders today, but it can be managed effectively when people, ideas, and talents are brought together to understand how best to cope with it.*

function as necessary evils that ensure that the school can open its doors
and fill its classrooms. This mindset can serve to erect formidable barriers
between them and their advancement peers.

To be sure, this silo mentality does not only exist among schools. Dr. Peter
Hawkins recently delivered an online seminar to executive coaches on this
topic. He spoke about how the days of the heroic CEO—the individual who
singlehandedly saves a corporation from falling over the fiscal cliff and restores
it to past glory—are over. The team, he said, is the king of the twenty-first-
century workplace. And that is an issue, because many companies do not
promote genuine teamwork, particularly across departments.

Today's challenges, said Hawkins, stem from the rapid rate of workplace
change, as well as what he called the Unholy Trinity: increased demands,
increased expectations, and decreased resources. Do more, at higher quality,
and at a lower cost. To combat these challenges, Hawkins suggests that there
need to be lots of learning and deep connections, a continued flow of thoughts
and ideas throughout organizations that bring people together to grapple with
issues, identify solutions, and build trust and efficacy.

As noted in chapter 29, change is a huge challenge for leaders today, but it can
be managed effectively when people, ideas, and talents are brought together
to understand how best to cope with it.

Leaders of departmental silos need to come together regularly to clarify their
underlying mission, goals, and objectives, and share information about their
experiences, observations, successes, and setbacks. This communication
will help both sides in their work and promote consistent, complimentary
messaging that is crucial to recruit, retain, and satisfy constituents.

SECTION 8

KEEPING THE
BALANCE

CHAPTER 41

Criticism Means You Matter

*You have enemies? Good. That means you've stood up
for something, sometime in your life.*
WINSTON S. CHURCHILL

~

One of the hardest things for leaders (and all people, for that matter) to deal with is criticism. We all want to be right, do right, and have others consistently agree with and admire us. But every leader who has been around for even a short while knows that criticism is part and parcel of their experience. There is simply no way of avoiding it.

Consider all of history's greatest leaders. Regardless of their era and role, every person that we would associate with positively changing the course of history was censured during his or her lifetime, often in scathing, relentless terms. It makes no difference whether they were people of great character or not. Nor did it matter if they were on the winning side of the argument or struggle. If they stood for a cause, led a nation, or advanced a noteworthy agenda, then they were at times discouraged, condemned, and perhaps even physically impeded in achieving their goals and aspirations.

Such thoughts can be sobering, if not outright disheartening. Why would anyone want to assume a leadership position when the potential for constant critique and pushback looms large? And why risk affecting relationships with friends, colleagues, coworkers, and other associates just to climb the corporate ladder?

The answer is simple. Besides the financial and status perks they receive in these posts, leaders believe in their mission and want to make a difference. They recognize that change is not easy for people and that their actions and decisions will invariably draw criticism. But they push forward anyway, knowing that criticism is simply other people's way of saying that what you're doing matters and deserves attention.

Of course, there are many things that leaders could and should do to gain support and buy-in, such as building equity, developing a values system, and communicating (and listening) well. All of these we have discussed above. Still, no leader who seeks to achieve anything meaningful can expect to adequately fulfill his or her responsibilities without experiencing some degree of criticism and backlash.

Let's imagine the following scenario. A CEO independently initiates a major change initiative at work. Moving forward, all international accounts will be closed so that the company can focus on its domestic clients. A memo is distributed to that effect, and then the boss announces it at the next company meeting. He waits for the fallout, expecting all sorts of pushback. To his utter surprise, there is none. Instead, he is met with absolute silence, as if nothing happened.

> *In the words of Churchill, "Criticism may not be agreeable, but it is necessary. It fulfils the same function as pain in the human body. It calls attention to an unhealthy state of things."*

How would the CEO feel in such a case? Perhaps he would worry that the conversation has gone underground. Maybe he would come to suspect that the complaints will arrive in another form. But if weeks go by and there is still no critical feedback on the matter from above or below, he would have to conclude that he, his initiative, or both, are simply irrelevant in others' eyes.

We're familiar with the philosophical question, "If a tree falls in a forest and no one is around to hear it, does it make a sound?" In modern business terms the question can perhaps be phrased as follows: "If a leader initiates change and no one comes forth to critique it, did it make a difference?"

It is not my purpose to explain *why* people criticize, though we can certainly list some common causes, including genuine disagreement, not wanting to be inconvenienced, and a desire to share a different set of ideas than what the leader is proposing. I simply want to remind every leader that *criticism is inevitable*—a thought that should hold profound meaning for everyone who is tasked to lead others.

Often, we confuse quiet with correctness and water-cooler chatter with error. We assume that if the rank and file are agitated, then we must have slipped up big-time and now need to shift into major damage control. This may be true at times. But it also may simply reflect the fact that what you are doing matters and impacts others in a profound way. Again, in the words of Churchill, "Criticism may not be agreeable, but it is necessary. It fulfils the same function as pain in the human body. It calls attention to an unhealthy state of things."

I sometimes think of change in terms of an inoculation. We inject a small vial of disease-causing agent into our bodies so that it can develop the necessary antibodies to survive a more robust invasion in the future. We may briefly enter into an unhealthy state of things, contracting fever and other side effects to emerge healthier for the long haul.

Change initiatives are in many ways similar. They can often start out as painful, affecting such things as staffing levels, roles, reporting, workloads, work processes, and the like. But often these changes are needed to ensure the long-term health of the organization.

Sure, leaders need to account for what they do, how they do it, and the impact that it may have on their constituents. But they must also possess the courage and drive to advance change that they believe is proper and necessary. The backlash that they will invariably receive is not necessarily the result of anything bad that they did; quite the contrary. It may, in fact, be the greatest indicator that they are on the right path and are genuinely doing what is necessary to fulfill their leadership duties.

CHAPTER 42

Would You Do This for Free?

A person can succeed at almost anything for which
they have unlimited enthusiasm.

CHARLES M. SCHWAB

~

I once attended an entrepreneurship event sponsored by a local university. The program allowed for each attendee to speak for a few minutes about his or her company and services. The last speaker was a videographer and web marketer. He spoke with great passion about finding a voice and telling a great story, important components in today's evolving marketplace. But the line that resonated most with me was his comment about why we are all doing what we're doing.

Most people in that room had left an established, more guaranteed position to venture off into entrepreneurship and follow their dreams. This speaker spoke to a common chord within each of us when he said, "you all love what you do so much that you would do it for free." That is, of course, if not for the fact that we must put food on the table.

Yes, I would do what I do for free if I could. You see, I am passionate about my work as an executive coach, much as I was about my previous work in the classroom and as a school leader. I have always believed strongly in making a difference in the lives of others, whether for children and those who inspire them or for leaders who seek to optimize and help their teams and organizations be the very best that they can be. So, if I did not have to concern myself with making a livelihood, I am sure that I would still seek ways to add value to others' lives and help them achieve their lofty goals.

We all appreciate meeting people who love what they do. Whether it's a store clerk, a postman, a doctor, a receptionist, or a corporate executive, we are lifted and inspired by people who are passionate about their jobs and seek to be a difference maker.

Nowhere is passion more important than in the leader's chair. Regardless of what field you work in, a leader needs to be someone who, to quote American president John Quincy Adams, "inspire(s) others to dream more, learn more, do more and become more."

What makes leader passion so important? For starters, passion is a primary predictor of success. In a book that they co-authored, authors Robert Kriegel and Louis Patler cite a fascinating study about passion.[61] The study looked at 1,500 people over a period of twenty years. At the study's outset, the population was divided into two groups. Group *A* comprised 83 percent of the sample. These folks were embarking on a career chosen for the purpose of making money now so that they could do what they really want to do in life at a later time. Group *B*, the remaining 17 percent of the sample, had chosen their career path for the opposite reason. They were going to pursue their passions immediately and concern themselves with money later.

Most people would likely predict that Group *A* would have seen more financial success than Group *B*. In fact, the exact opposite happened. Of the 1,500 participants, 101 had become millionaires during the twenty years of the study. All but one of those millionaires was from Group *B*—the ones who had chosen to pursue what they loved not only had more fun but enjoyed greater affluence.

How exactly did this happen? The answer, it seems, is passion. Group *A* focused on the process. What steps can I take to live a financially rewarding life? There was little fun in the process, however, and this limited their careers. In contrast, nearly 40 percent of the folks who set out to enjoy their lives and find work that connected deeply with their passions became millionaires.

When you love what you do, it becomes easier to do it. It also becomes easier to sell it. Simon Sinek famously said, "people don't buy what you do; they buy why you do it." They want to buy your passion as much as your product.

Passion is good for other things as well, such as:

- **Energy.** Passion produces energy, which drives us forward. President Donald Trump once said, "Without passion, you don't have energy; without energy, you have nothing."

---

[61] Kriegel, Robert J., and Louis Patler. *If It Ain't Broke—Break It! And Other Unconventional Wisdom for a Changing Business World*. New York: Warner Books, 1991.

- **Vision.** Passions fuel our visions and dreams. They also help us communicate them in a way that is clear and vivid.

- **Impact.** We all know the impact that passionate people have on those around them. Their passion rubs off on the rest in a way that makes them feel more energized and motivated.

- **Opportunity.** A leader's passion can bring new opportunity and open the door to success. People want to be with and work with others who bring their very selves to the workplace and/or the discussion.

- **Followers.** When a leader is passionate, people feel a deep sense of being led in a worthy direction by someone who is committed to something more important than his or her individual glory. This is the kind of person that they want to follow.

What do passionate people look like? Passionate people act in support of their passion. This means that they walk their talk and ensure that their day-to-day behaviors are consistent with their beliefs and drives. They express their message in a manner that demonstrates conviction and hunger to meet objectives. They also remain committed to their goals despite adversity and setbacks. When difficulties arise, they hold strong to their principles and find a way forward.

Passionate people counteract their frustration by focusing on what is going right and what is working now, in contrast to what is falling apart or not going as planned. They do not get sidetracked by daily challenges because they believe they have control over their situation.

People who are passionate have an energy about them that draws people to them and makes others want to emulate them, to get what they've got. Their passion is contagious. Leaders, in particular, can create an enjoyable workplace environment in which people look forward to coming in to work every day and being part of the organization's vision for the future. Passionate leaders tell a compelling story that catches the attention of people and guide them to see it, feel it, and envision the future. Leaders who are passionate feel unstoppable. Their passion has a trickle-down effect and can be a secret ingredient to your company's success, particularly in a world of intense business competition.

Passion loves company. Passionate leaders know this and involve their people in their passion. They know they must have faith in and empower others for people to be passionate about what needs to be accomplished. To help them succeed, passionate leaders surround themselves with enthusiastic, knowledgeable team members who can provide insightful ideas and concrete suggestions that the leader may not have thought of.

CHAPTER 43

Establish Clear Work-Home Boundaries

Don't confuse having a career with having a life.
HILLARY RODHAM CLINTON

One of the biggest challenges for any leader is to establish clear boundaries separating work from home. Many people fall into the trap of not setting boundaries regularly, making their homes extensions of the office. While doing so may make sense or feel right at the moment, this can have negative repercussions, particularly if done regularly.

Even if you love your job and approach it each day with passion and purpose (which I hope you do!), work can still be stressful, exhausting, and all-consuming. When you bring it home with you, it encroaches upon your needed relaxation time. It also takes away from the family/social time that is so crucial. At the least, it may put you in a foul, crabby mood, affecting your job performance.

How can leaders avoid falling into the blurred-lines trap so that they can get the relaxation and quality personal time they need and deserve?

Begin this process before your workday formally ends. As you near its conclusion, make a list of projects you still need to complete, in order of priority. If not enough time remains in the current workday, map out how you will address these tasks as soon as possible on the next day. Review this list at the beginning of each workday and work towards its completion.

Regarding late day e-mails, consider leaving them for the next day. Phone calls can go to voice-mail, which you can check just to make sure that there's nothing urgent. In those cases, you will respond accordingly. If the message is not pressing, resolve to take care of it the following day.

As you walk in the front door after work, be careful not to bring along any problems that will impact your time at home. One way to do this is to hang a "problem hook" by the front door, as illustrated by the following story.

Once, there was a young father who was unemployed. A kind old man saw an opportunity to help him. He asked the young man if would like to bring his tools and spend a few days working on repairing an old fence he had around his large property. The young man readily agreed.

The young father had less than a productive first day. His old truck broke down about two miles from the old man's house, forcing him to walk. He arrived forty-five minutes late. Then the hammer that he had brought broke about half-way through the day. To make matters worse, he severely twisted his ankle towards the end of the day and could barely walk.

The kind old man offered him a ride home. When they had almost reached the house, the young father invited him in to meet his family. As the two men approached the rickety door of the humble home the tired, beat-down worker paused on the porch and touched a large coat hook with both of his hands. When opening the door, the young father completely transformed. A big broad smile came across his face as he hugged his three small, happy children and kissed his wife.

Later, as the young man escorted his guest out the door, they again passed the large coat hook. The old man's curiosity got the better of him, and he asked his worker about what he had seen him do earlier. He was told as follows: "That's my problem hook. I know I am going to have problems, but one thing I never want to do is bring them home to my wife and children. So I simply hang my problems on the hook before I enter my house. When I leave in the morning, I pick them up again." The young father continued. "The odd thing about it is when I pick them up in the morning they don't seem to be as big and heavy as they were when I dropped them off the night before."

Whether you choose to hang an actual reminder or just identify a figurative one (such as the threshold of your home), such symbolism can help erect an absolute barrier between your work experience and what lies behind the front door of your home. Why subject your family to the challenges and stressors from the past ten hours of your day? As you enter, think about the new opportunities you will have to connect with those whom you love.

Even better, identify the best thing that happened that day and share it right as you enter, even if it was just a good cup of coffee or the fact that the train arrived on time.

If you are completely wound up and need time to decompress, give your spouse a heads-up and spend a few minutes alone at first. Some activities that can help you relax include resting, meditation, exercise, or a warm shower.

> *As you walk in the front door after work, be careful not to bring along any problems that will impact your time at home. One way to do this is to hang a "problem hook" by the front door.*

Of course, not everyone has the luxury of completely shutting down after hours. In that case, try to plan with your team at work how to minimize the impact of such intrusions. But don't invite such invasions by checking work e-mail or doing other work-related tasks that can wait until the morning.

When you feel the itch to jump back into work mode, I suggest that you consider the wise words of Steve Blank, author of *The Startup Owner's Manual*. Blank wrote, "When you're gone would you rather have your gravestone say, 'He never missed a meeting' or one that said, 'He was a great father'?"[62]

---

[62] Blank, Steven G., and Bob Dorf. *The Startup Owner's Manual: The Step-by-Step Guide for Building a Great Company.* Pescadero, CA: K&S Ranch, 2012.

CHAPTER 44

Walking the Tightrope of Life

*Happiness is not a matter of intensity but of balance,
order, rhythm and harmony.*

THOMAS MERTON

~

Many of us, particularly busy leaders, struggle to achieve and maintain proper balance in our lives. We seek to succeed in the work arena while simultaneously being there for our families and loved ones. We have a strong sense of community and want to give back to those around us while also ensuring that we attend to our emotional, spiritual, and health-related needs on a regular basis.

Despite our best intentions, however, these many aims often come into direct conflict with one another. We simply cannot allot as much time as we would like to each of these areas in a manner that is fully satisfying. We need to recognize this well before we become consumed by stress and/or guilt.

So how can we manage to strike the proper balance between these oft-competing realms in a manner that is both responsible and fulfilling?

A story is told about an American businessman, who was on vacation in Mexico. While at the beach, he saw a local fisherman docking at the shore with many fish in tow. The American complimented the fisherman on his catch and asked him how long it took him to catch that many fish.

"Not long, a couple of hours."

"So why didn't you stay out longer and catch more?" asked the tourist.

"Because this is enough for my family and me," he was told.

The businessman persisted. "So what do you do with the rest of your time?"

"I sleep late, fish for a while, play with my children, take a siesta and spend time with my wife," said the fisherman. "In the evening, I go into the village to visit my friends. I have a few drinks, play the guitar and sing a few songs. I have a full life."

The American couldn't believe his ears. "I am a successful businessman, and I can help you," he said. "You should spend more time on the water fishing. You can sell the extra fish, make more money, and buy a bigger boat."

Fisherman: "And after that?"

"Use the extra money made from the bigger boat," said the businessman. "To buy a few boats and hire more people to operate a fleet of fishing vessels."

"All of this fish will give you market leverage. Instead of selling your fish to a middle man, you can start to negotiate directly with the buyers. After a while, you would be able to open your own plant. Then you could leave this little village for Mexico City and maybe even New York. From there you could operate the whole business."

"How long would that take?" asked the fisherman.

"Somewhere between twenty to twenty-five years," came the reply.

"What next?"

"Well, that's when the fun starts," explained the tourist. "When the business gets really big, you can sell stock in the company and make millions!"

"Wow, millions. This is getting interesting. What happens after I earn millions?" asked the fisherman.

"After that, you'll be able to retire on the coast, sleep in every day, do some fishing, play with your grandkids, take a siesta and spend time with your wife. In the evenings, you will be able to go out drinking and singing with your friends."

The fisherman just shrugged his shoulders and walked away.

As this story simply illustrates, too many folks have confused priorities, or at least lose out on the means in their quest to enjoy the ends. We all know that life is about more than money, perks, and notoriety. We have to be able to live, not just work. And for too many of us, this crucial balance gets lost in the rat race.

Folks with strong work-life balance:

- **Lead purposeful lives.** Balanced people give serious thought to how they want to live their lives. They develop and then commit to a road map that will help them get there.

- **Adjust as needed.** Like most things in life, well-conceived plans can easily go sideways if we let them. People who stay on track continually ponder and dialogue about what is working or not, and adjust as needed.

- **Carve out time.** It's one thing to say that things outside of work are important to you. It's another to make the time for those things. Purposeful people don't wait to see what time is left over after work. They make a point of planning and booking time off to spend outside of work and carefully guard this time.

- **Develop personal definitions of success.** People who have strong work-life balance have a clear vision of what success looks and feels like. They use that to pursue their goals with greater purpose and discipline.

- **Turn off all distractions.** Today more than ever, it is easy to become distracted. Our phones and other technology sidetrack us from what's important and what needs to get done. People with clear priorities can turn off their devices to focus and achieve their goals. They prioritize the need to for quality uninterrupted time to do the things that they enjoy.

> *We all know that life is about more than money, perks, and notoriety. We have to be able to live, not just work.*

- **Tap into their spiritual sides.** Often lost in the workplace shuffle is our need for spiritual connectivity. Religion, meditation, or other spiritual outlets offer an element of fulfillment and purpose that keep us going and recharge our souls.

- **Engage in relaxing and rejuvenating activities.** Balanced people know the importance of "sharpening the saw."[63] They use music, yoga, physical activity, hobbies, or other interests that allow them to get away from the pressures of everyday life to regenerate themselves.

- **Hold short- and long-term views.** Some people have a clear sense of what a balanced life looks like, but feel a need to put such thinking on hold for the short-term as they get through school or get their business off of the ground. They set time frames for when they expect to transition into a more balanced lifestyle and then hold themselves accountable to that time frame, adjusting as needed.

To achieve balance it is critical that we take the time to identify and prioritize our core values and aspirations. Often this is best achieved through the creation of a personal mission statement, which helps you to lay out what is most important to you and pinpoint what you want to achieve in each realm. A coach, guide, or mentor can be helpful here in asking the hard questions that drill down on what is truly critical and a priority.

Here are some examples of personal mission statements from established leaders:[64]

- *"To serve as a leader, live a balanced life, and apply ethical principles to make a significant difference."* —Denise Morrison, CEO of Campbell Soup Company

- *"To have fun in [my] journey through life and learn from [my] mistakes."* —Sir Richard Branson, founder of The Virgin Group

- *"To be a teacher. And to be known for inspiring my students to be more than they thought they could be."* —Oprah Winfrey, founder of OWN, the Oprah Winfrey Network

---

[63] Covey, Stephen R. *The Seven Habits of Highly Effective People: Restoring the Character Ethic.* New York: Simon and Schuster, 1989: 287. Stephen Covey called this "sharpening the saw" (a reference to taking care of yourself) so that the lumberjack (leader) could continue to cut down trees (by having the energy and drive to lead and influence change).

[64] Vozza, Stephanie. "Personal Mission Statements Of 5 Famous CEOs (And Why You Should Write One Too)." *Fast Company.* February 25, 2014. Accessed February 22, 2017. https://www.fastcompany.com/3026791/dialed/personal-mission-statements-of-5-famous-ceos-and-why-you-should-write-one-too.

Once you arrive at some answers, you can compare it to your present reality. Keep tabs on how you currently use your time and compare that data with what's truly important to you. Use this insight to make adjustments to your schedule and in how you prioritize your daily activities.

Not only will this process offer you a fresh new focus and a revitalized sense of purpose, but it will also strengthen your self-identity. Self-identity emerges from the way that you see yourself. What makes you tick? What is most important to you, and how does that affect your decision-making? Knowing who you are at your core can be extremely empowering and allow you to forge ahead despite the inevitable challenges that arise. As the great developmental psychologist, Erik Erikson, once said, "In the social jungle of human existence, there is no feeling of being alive without a sense of identity."[65]

You may be tempted to tuck your values list away for personal reference. I strongly suggest, however, that you share it with those that they impact most. Let them know what you consider most when making decisions. Giving others around you a window into how you value and budget your time can help them better understand your actions and appreciate your perspective.

Another important consideration for leaders is to be careful to avoid burnout. Burnout can occur quickly when leaders fail to maintain proper balance and act in a manner that is unhealthy and unsustainable. Take good care of yourself by eating well, getting enough sleep, and taking regular vacation breaks from the daily grind.

We all struggle to make proper use of our time and energies. We want to be as successful, as helpful, and as accomplished as possible in every important domain. But we simply cannot do everything. It is critical to find ways to manage the ongoing conflict that exists between competing domains in a way that helps us to feel most fulfilled.

---

[65] Erikson, Erik H. *Identity, Youth, and Crisis*. New York: W.W. Norton, 1968: 38.

CHAPTER 45

It's Lonely at the Top

The price of leadership is loneliness...I think it is inescapable.
GORDON B. HINCKLEY

~

One of the most famous American photos was captured by reporter George Tames on February 10, 1961. The picture is of President John F. Kennedy, recently inaugurated, standing hunched over in the Oval Office. From behind, it looks as if he is carrying the weight of the world on his shoulders. Kennedy, who had a bad back, was simply reading the newspaper standing up, as he often preferred to do. Still, the image, which the *New York Times* would later christen, "The loneliest job in the world," would take on greater significance as Kennedy navigated through the Cuban Missile Crisis and other global challenges.

~

Loneliness is, in a relative sense, measured in the eyes of the beholder. Some argue that the loneliest professionals in the world are those who toil in isolation, with limited opportunity for interpersonal communication. These include writers, poets, and scientific researchers working in remote outposts.

There are others who weigh loneliness not by the frequency or infrequency of their interactions with others but rather with the quality of such exchanges. Therapists, for example, often feel lonely, despite the many deep conversations that they have on an average day. Since they tend to spend so much of their time listening and giving to others, they do not benefit from the balanced conversation and idea exchange that meets their own social needs.

The same could be said for teachers. I once read a book that posited that classroom teaching was the world's loneliest position. The author argued that teachers were required to go into isolated classrooms each day and spend many hours alone with students—hardly a satisfying set of social

partners. They often have little time
to chat with peers and even less time
engaging in meaningful learning
and problem-solving activities with
colleagues.

As a former classroom teacher, I
know that it can feel lonely at times to
occupy your day communicating with
others who are not your peers and
who cannot relate to your experiences
and passions. Still, I suggest that the

> *Learn to distinguish between loneliness and solitude. Paul Tillich once said, "Loneliness expresses the pain of being alone and solitude expresses the glory of being alone."*

loneliest job may very well be that of a leader, whether it's the leader of the
free world, a school principal, or a CEO.

Most employees have others in the workplace that they can turn to for
advice, feedback and/or companionship. They can ask questions about how
to get things done and work through tough times with their peers without
unreasonable concern that they will be unnecessarily or unfavorably judged
(or worse). They can share a joke in the office, fill their March Madness
brackets, and comfortably discuss what's going on in their personal lives.
They can also spend time with their associates after work, as a natural
extension of their time together in the office.

Leaders, on the other hand, have fewer people to turn to when things
get tough. Who in the organization, after all, has to sign off on the types
of decisions that they must make each day? It can certainly be difficult to
confide in and bare their souls to direct reports. And those who sit above
them in the corporate or organizational food chain (such as the chairman of
the board) are also not the ones to whom they want to display weakness or
vulnerability.

Furthermore, it can be awkward and inappropriate for bosses to try to
chum up with their coworkers. Sure, there's nothing wrong with occasional
outside-of-work interaction. Many times it can be both fun and healthy and
offer all parties the chance to see each other in a different light. But at the
end of the day, the boss is the boss, and that still spells social isolation for the
guy calling the shots.

For these reasons, I strongly advocate leader participation in peer learning/ advisory groups. Not only do such settings provide leaders with meaningful learning opportunities to strengthen their skills and augment their toolkits, but they also offer safe havens for leaders to open up about problems to others who can relate to their struggles and provide concrete suggestions, if not solutions. Often, these business groups also develop into social relationships that add balance to the lives of high-powered execs.

Leaders should also make time to attend classes and training with members of their executive team and board of directors. Learning together and sharing ideas in a neutral setting can open up pathways towards deeper bonding that may not otherwise occur.

Of course, there are other ways to reduce feelings of loneliness, such as having a strong network of family and friends to turn to outside the office. Hiring a coach or therapist can also help fill a social void (in addition to the other benefits that they offer), as can networking events, dinner parties, social clubs, religious congregations, and volunteering in the community. In the words of Dorothy Day: "We have all known the long loneliness, and we have found that the answer is community."

Collect inspirational quotes and thank you letters for when you need them. Read thought-provoking books about leadership as well as personal accounts of triumph and success. Many authors possess the gift of connecting with their words and building community through the printed or digital page.

Lastly, learn to distinguish between loneliness and solitude. Paul Tillich once said, "Loneliness expresses the pain of being alone and solitude expresses the glory of being alone." Being alone is only a problem when we need others to fill the void of silence. Leaders who can dig deep within themselves for insight and self-encouragement will find the isolated time of solitude to be the most clarifying, purifying, and rewarding time that they have in their busy, hectic schedules.

CHAPTER 46
It's What You Make of It

Leadership is the ability to not only understand and utilize your innate talents, but to also effectively leverage the natural strengths of your team to accomplish the mission. There is no one-size-fits-all approach, answer key or formula to leadership. Leadership should be the humble, authentic expression of your unique personality in pursuit of bettering whatever environment you are in.

KATIE CHRISTY, FOUNDER, ACTIVATE YOUR TALENT

~

A parable is told about a pencil maker who was preparing to put an important pencil in a box. Before doing so, though, he took the pencil aside. "There are five things you need to know," he said. "If you can remember these five things, you will become the best pencil you can be."

1. You will be able to do many great things, but only if you allow yourself to be held in someone else's hand.

2. Sharpening is painful, but it is critical if you want to write sharply.

3. Since you have an eraser, you can correct most mistakes you make, though some may be harder to erase than others.

4. Remember, it's what's inside that's most important.

5. Whatever surface you are used on, make sure you leave your mark. No matter how hard, rough, or easy, you must continue to write.

This parable shares powerful lessons for every leader, many of which we have discussed throughout this book.

1. **Be humble.** You can achieve greatness, but not when you go it alone. Allow yourself to be taught and coached by others and identify the strengths of those around you to help advance the cause.

2. **Stay sharp.** Strong leaders find ways to keep learning and sharpening their skills. Feedback can be painful at times, but without it, you will become dull.

3. **Accept mistakes.** We all err. Though mistakes may make for challenging moments, they are ultimately part of a process of becoming a better leader. Embrace your mistakes as opportunities to learn, erase, and become better! As John Maxwell once said, "A good leader is a person who takes a little more than his share of the blame and a little less than his share of the credit."

4. **Your best is what's inside you.** You may be good-looking, dress well, and have a great personality. But what makes you who you are and the person with whom others want to connect is your character. Seek to continually grow and refine your character so that you can lead and serve with utmost integrity.

5. **Stick with it.** There will be times when you think that you're making no imprint and that your actions are not having an effect. But people will still depend on you, so you need to keep on going. Hold to your vision and your dreams, even when it seems they have dimmed.

~

Throughout this book, I have attempted to offer guidance to you, the new leader, as you assume your leadership position. By now, one thing should be clear: leadership is not easy. It takes much effort to position yourself to achieve a leadership post, and perhaps, even more, work to build a sustainable leadership platform.

But it is doable. And the world needs you.

In a 1913 address to students at Swarthmore College, Woodrow Wilson said, "You are not here merely to make a living. You are here to enable the world to live more amply, with greater vision, with a finer spirit of hope and achievement. You are here to enrich the world, and you impoverish yourself if you forget the errand."

The fact that you have been promoted into leadership means that you have the tools and energy to make it happen. Things will get in your way, but if you continue to believe in yourself, you can become the leader that everyone around you hopes that you will be.

Leadership blogger and Minister Brian Dodd summarized the roles and opportunities of a leader as follows:[66]

1. Leaders provide vision and offer direction.

2. Leaders believe in others and give them confidence.

3. Leaders stretch others' thinking and make them look at things differently.

4. Leaders sharpen others' skills and help them become better at what they do.

5. Leaders support others and provide what is needed to be successful.

6. Leaders make hard decisions. They pay the price, so others don't have to.

7. Leaders take the bullets and bear responsibility.

8. Leaders create experiences that help others see things in a new and different light.

9. Leaders raise others' self-image and make them feel better about themselves.

These are many of the opportunities that leaders have each day to impact those around them.

As much as I have endeavored to support you in your leadership journey, it bears repeating that there is no one-size-fits-all approach, answer key or formula to leadership. Each leader finds his or her way to the top and must determine what style and approach best suits him or her, as illustrated by

---

[66] Adapted from "The Top 10 Benefits Of Leadership." Brian Dodd on Leadership. October 26, 2012. Accessed February 22, 2017. http://briandoddonleadership.com/2011/04/28/thetop-10-benefits-of-leadership/.

this powerful story.[67]

High in the Himalayan Mountains lived a wise old man. Every so often, he ventured down into the nearby village to entertain the locals with his special knowledge and talents. One of his skills was to use psychic powers to tell the villagers the contents in their pockets, boxes, or minds.

A few young boys from the village decided to play a joke on the wise old man and discredit his special abilities. One boy decided that he would capture a bird and hide it in his hands. He knew, of course, that the wise old man would know that the object in his hands was a bird.

> *It bears repeating that there is no one-size-fits-all approach, answer key or formula to leadership. Each leader finds his or her way to the top and must determine what style and approach best suits him or her.*

The boy came up with a plan. He would ask the old man if the bird was dead or alive. If the wise man said the bird was alive, the boy would crush the bird in his hands and kill it. If the wise man said the bird was dead, the boy would open his hands and let the bird fly free. In this way, the boy would prove the old man to be a fraud.

The following week, the wise old man came down from the mountain into the village. The boy quickly caught a bird. Cupping it out of sight in his hands, he walked up to the wise old man and asked, "Old man, what do I have in my hands?"

The wise old man said, "You have a bird," and he was right.

The boy then asked, "Old man, old man tell me, is the bird alive or is it dead?"

The wise old man looked at the boy and said, "The bird is as you choose it."

This is the essence of your new leadership journey. The path that you take and your ultimate destiny are in your hands. The question is, what will you do with your opportunity?

---

[67] From Hyatt, Michael S., and Daniel Harkavy. *Living Forward: A Proven Plan to Stop Drifting and Get the Life You Want*. Grand Rapids, MI: Baker Books, 2016.

About the Author

~

Naphtali Hoff, PsyD, is president of Impactful Coaching & Consulting. He is an executive coach, organizational consultant, and sought-after trainer and lecturer. He holds two masters degrees in education and educational leadership, respectively, and completed his doctorate in human and organizational psychology.

Naphtali's passion for leadership began during his leadership journey, which included administrative posts in multiple schools. His personal experience in the leadership field allows him to understand leaders' needs and craft solutions to help them optimize their performance and success.

To inquire about bulk book discounts or booking Naphtali Hoff as a speaker, please send an e-mail to author@becomingthenewboss.com or call 212-470-6139.

ACKNOWLEDGMENTS

I begin with deepest appreciation to my wife and life partner, Karyn. You have been with me through thick and thin, and were my rock and support throughout all of my leadership journeys. You allowed me to pursue them even when they took us away from family and friends and made things challenging for our family. I could never have done it—or written this—without you.

To each of my children: Binyomin, Doniel, Shaina, Chaim, Malka, and Anshel. Leadership starts at home and you challenge me each day to be the very best leader of our family that I can be. To Binyomin, Doniel, Shaina, and Chaim: thank you for allowing me to be your principal and for gracefully tolerating the challenges that came with being the principal's kid.

My parents: David and Judy Hoff, and Katherine Hoff. You gave me the foundation that I needed to attack life head on and the grit and tenacity to overcome challenges along the way. Thank you for loving, teaching, and supporting me all through the years.

My in-laws, Susan Feuer and Dr. Lawrence Perl: You raised a great daughter and have supported us in so many ways. Our kids really appreciate their relationship with you.

Rabbi Dr. Leonard Matanky: You gave me my first teaching opportunity and I have never looked back. You also showed me how to succeed at leadership.

Rabbi Moshe Yosef Ungar: Working at the Cheder allowed me to spread my wings and develop so many of my leadership skills. Your warmth, patience, and guidance will remain with me forever.

Rabbi Elisha Klausner: Working with you across the aisle could not have been more pleasant or rewarding. Your support and friendship were a true blessing.

Mark Gutman: Becoming rabbis together was a true highlight in my life. I cherish your friendship and admire your erudition.

To the Board of Directors and Faculty of TDSA: Thank you for giving me the opportunity to lead your school. I grew so much from my time in Atlanta and could never have written this book without the rich learning experiences from our time together.

Naomi May and Linda Rabinowitz: Thank you for taking me under your wings and showing me the ropes. You were there when I needed advice or a sounding board to bounce ideas off of.

My "chevra" at Yesud Maaloh: I learned so much with and from you. You were great study partners and even better friends.

Dr. Shani Bechhofer: You came down to Atlanta at my behest to help us cut through the weeds and get aligned. Thanks for showing me the impact that a talented consultant can have on an organization.

Dr. Arnie Dalkhe: As my professor and dissertation committee chair you were a true inspiration to me. You showed me what leadership looks like as we navigated through the challenging research and writing processes. Thanks as well to committee members Drs. Chris Ewing and Godwin Igein and program founder Dr. Michael Hamlin for your continued encouragement, support, and insights.

Henry DeVries of Indie Books International: My editor (together with the talented Denise Montgomery), publisher, and advisor. Thank you, Henry, for believing in this project and for giving me the support and direction needed to get it done. Thank you as well to Devin DeVries for skillfully navigating the publishing process.

Finally, and by no means the least deserving, to my Creator for bestowing upon me a blessed life filled with so many riches. My only hope is to use those gifts properly to add value, purpose, and inspiration to the lives that I am blessed to touch.

Works Referenced

Bennis, Warren G. *On Becoming a Leader*. Reading, MA: Addison-Wesley Pub., 1989.

Blanchard, Kenneth H., Cynthia Olmstead, and Martha C. Lawrence. *Trust Works! Four Keys to Building Lasting Relationships*. New York: William Morrow, 2013.

Blanchard, Ken, and Scott Blanchard. "Do Your Employees Trust You?" *Fast Company*. April 26, 2013. Accessed February 22, 2017. http://www.fastcompany.com/3008858/do-your-employees-trust-you.

Blank, Steve, and Bob Dorf. *The Step-by-Step Guide for Building a Great Company*. Pescadero, CA: K&S Ranch, 2012.

Bloom, Barry M. "Barry M. Bloom: Following Joe Torre, Manager Joe Girardi Able to Also Succeed with Yankees." Major League Baseball. February 18, 2014. Accessed February 22, 2017. http://m.mlb.com/news/article/67892380/barry-m-bloom-following-joe-torre-manager-joe-girardi-able-to-also-succeed-with-yankees/.

Building Trust. Performed by James Davis. TED Talks. December 6, 2014. Accessed February 22, 2017. https://youtu.be/s9FBK4eprmA.

"Change Management: Why 70% of Change Initiatives Fail." New Directions Consulting. Accessed February 22, 2017. http://newdirectionsconsulting.com/4639/blog/why-70-of-change-initiatives-fail-2/.

Collins, James C. *Good to Great: Why Some Companies Make the Leap...and Others Don't*. New York, NY: Harper Business, 2001.

Covey, Stephen R. *The Seven Habits of Highly Effective People: Restoring the Character Ethic*. New York: Simon and Schuster, 1989.

Dweck, Carol S. *Mindset: The New Psychology of Success*. New York: Random House, 2006.

Erikson, Erik H. *Identity, Youth, and Crisis*. New York: W.W. Norton, 1968.

"Executive Blind Spots." Hay Group RSS. Accessed February 22, 2017. http://www.haygroup.com/us/downloads/details.aspx?id=7347.

"Finding the First Rung." DDI International. Accessed February 22, 2017. http://www.ddiworld.com/resources/library/trend-research/finding-the-first-rung.

First Why and Then Trust. Performed by Scott Sinek. TED Talks. April 6, 2011. Accessed February 22, 2017. https://youtu.be/4VdO7LuoBzM.

Gallup, Inc. "U.S. Workers Remain Largely Satisfied With Their Jobs." Gallup.com. November 27, 2007. Accessed February 22, 2017. http://www.gallup.com/poll/102898/us-workers-remain-largely-satisfied-their-jobs.aspx.

Goleman, Daniel. *Emotional Intelligence*. New York: Bantam Books, 1995.

Guthrie, Doug. "Creative Leadership: Humility and Being Wrong." *Forbes*. June 06, 2012. Accessed February 22, 2017. http://www.forbes.com/sites/dougguthrie/2012/06/01/creative-leadership-humility-and-being-wrong/.

Hyatt, Michael S., and Daniel Harkavy. *Living Forward: A Proven Plan to Stop Drifting and Get the Life You Want*. Grand Rapids, MI: Baker Books, 2016.

"Jigsaw Groups for Cooperative Learning: Teaching Strategy for Students (Grades K-12)." Teaching Strategy for Students (Grades K-12) - TeacherVision. Accessed February 22, 2017. https://www.teachervision.com/group-work/cooperative-learning/48532.html?detoured=1.

"Job Satisfaction: 2014 Edition." The Conference Board. Accessed February 22, 2017. http://www.conference-board.org/publications/publicationdetail.cfm?publicationid=2785.

Walsh, Ken. "The First 100 Days Franklin Roosevelt." *US News &World Report*, December 2, 2009.

Kotter, John P. *Leading Change*. Boston, MA: Harvard Business School Press, 1996.

Kotter, John P. "Management Is (Still) Not Leadership." *Harvard Business Review.* August 07, 2014. Accessed February 22, 2017. http://blogs.hbr.org/2013/01/management-is-still-not-leadership/.

Kotter, John P. "On Becoming A Leader." In *Leading Change.* Boston, MA: Harvard Business School Press, 1996.

Kriegel, Robert J., and Louis Patler. *If It Ain't Broke—Break It! And Other Unconventional Wisdom for a Changing Business World.* New York: Warner Books, 1991.

Kruger, Justin, Nicholas Epley, Jason Parker, and Zhi-Wen Ng. "Egocentrism over E-mail: Can We Communicate as Well as We Think?" *Journal of Personality and Social Psychology* 89, no. 6 (2005): 925-36. doi:10.1037/0022-3514.89.6.925.

"The Law of Buy-In." Horeb International. October 11, 2012. Accessed February 22, 2017. http://www.horebinternational.com/the-law-of-buy-in/.

Linking Silos: Academic Leadership and Institutional Advancement. Naphtali Hoff. April 26, 2015. Accessed February 22, 2017. https://youtu.be/e4qJTawMhgw.

Maxwell, John C. *The Five Levels of Leadership: Proven Steps to Maximize Your Potential.* New York: Center Street, 2011.

Morris, Rhett. "Mentors Are The Secret Weapons Of Successful Startups." *TechCrunch.* Accessed February 22, 2017. https://techcrunch.com/2015/03/22/mentors-are-the-secret-weapons-of-successful-startups/.

"Paradigms." *Leaders Are Readers.* July 20, 2010. Accessed February 22, 2017. https://goeagle.wordpress.com/tag/paradigm/.

"Passion at Work." DU Press. Accessed February 22, 2017. http://dupress.com/articles/worker-passion-employee-behavior/.

Paula, Ramona. "Pwc Internal Change Capability." Scribd. Accessed February 22, 2017. https://www.scribd.com/document/177117495/Pwc-Internal-Change-Capability.

Rath, Tom, and Donald O. Clifton. *How Full Is Your Bucket? Positive Strategies for Work and Life.* New York: Gallup Press, 2004.

Rath, Tom. *Strengths Finder 2.0*. New York: Gallup Press, 2007.

"ReTHINK: Interview with Robin Sharma." GeniusTribes Training Resources. Accessed February 22, 2017. http://rethink-redefine.blogspot.com/2012/10/rethink-interview-with-robin-sharma.html.

Shaw, Robert B. *Leadership Blindspots: How Successful Leaders Identify and Overcome the Weaknesses That Matter*. Wiley, 2014.

"Shinobu Ishizuka: 2 Lessons from Japan's Values-Driven Companies." Benedictine University CVDL. September 01, 2015. Accessed February 22, 2017. http://www.cvdl.org/blog/shinobu-ishizuka-2-lessons-japans-values-driven-companies/.

Sinek, Simon. *Leaders Eat Last: Why Some Teams Pull Together and Others Don't*. Kbh.: Nota, 2014.

Strack, Rainer, Carsten Von Der Linden, Mike Booker, and Andrea Strohmeyer. "Decoding Global Talent." www.bcgperspectives.com. October 06, 2014. Accessed February 22, 2017. https://www.bcgperspectives.com/content/articles/human_resources_leadership_decoding_global_talent/

"Think, Pair, Share Cooperative Learning Strategy: For Teachers (Grades K-12)." TeacherVision. Accessed February 22, 2017. https://www.teachervision.com/group-work/cooperative-learning/48547.html.

Thompson, Mark. "How Top Leaders Handle Setbacks and Criticism." Inc.com. June 06, 2014. Accessed February 22, 2017. http://www.inc.com/mark-thompson/how-to-survive-criticism.html.

Tichy, Noel M., and Eli B. Cohen. *The Leadership Engine: How Winning Companies Build Leaders at Every Level*. New York, NY: Harper Business, 1997.

"The Top 10 Benefits Of Leadership." Brian Dodd on Leadership. October 26, 2012. Accessed February 22, 2017. http://briandoddonleadership.com/2011/04/28/thetop-10-benefits-of-leadership/.

The Top 10 Mistakes of Entrepreneurs. Produced by Berkeley-Haas. Performed by Guy Kawasaki. March 7, 2013. Accessed February 22, 2017. https://youtu.be/HHjgK6p4nrw.

Vozza, Stephanie. "Personal Mission Statements Of 5 Famous CEOs (And

Why You Should Write One Too)." *Fast Company*. February 25, 2014. Accessed February 22, 2017. https://www.fastcompany.com/3026791/dialed/personal-mission-statements-of-5-famous-ceos-and-why-you-should-write-one-too.

Walker, Keith, and Bob Bayles. *Reflections on Facilitating Learning in Prairie Spirit*. Saskatoon: Turning Point Global, 2016.

Watkins, Michael. *The First 90 Days: Critical Success Strategies for New Leaders at All Levels*. Boston, MA: Harvard Business School Press, 2003.

"What Are Your Values?: Deciding What's Most Important in Life." Decision-Making Skills from MindTools.com. Accessed February 22, 2017. http://www.mindtools.com/pages/article/newTED_85.htm.

Whitten, Neal. *Managing Software Development Projects: Formula for Success*. New York: Wiley, 1990.

Zaleznik, Abraham. "Managers and Leaders: Are They Different?" *Clinical Leadership & Management Review: The Journal of CLMA* 18, no. 3 (2004): 171.

Zenger, John H., Joseph R. Folkman, Robert H. Jr. Sherwin, and Barbara A. Steel. *How to Be Exceptional: Drive Leadership Success by Magnifying Your Strengths*. New York: McGraw-Hill, 2012.

Made in the USA
Columbia, SC
20 May 2018